Course

# TORT
# LAW

Brendan Greene

COURSE NOTES

**HODDER**
EDUCATION
AN HACHETTE UK COMPANY

Orders: please contact Bookpoint Ltd, 130 Milton Park, Abingdon, Oxon OX14 4SB. Telephone: (44) 01235 827720. Fax: (44) 01235 400454. Lines are open from 9.00 - 5.00, Monday to Saturday, with a 24 hour message answering service. You can also order through our website www.hoddereducation.co.uk

If you have any comments to make about this, or any of our other titles, please send them to educationenquiries@hodder.co.uk

*British Library Cataloguing in Publication Data*
A catalogue record for this title is available from the British Library

ISBN: 978 1 444 14656 1

First Edition Published 2012
Impression number    10 9 8 7 6 5 4 3 2 1
Year                 2015 2014 2013 2012

Hachette UK's policy is to use papers that are natural, renewable and recyclable products and made from wood grown in sustainable forests. The logging and manufacturing processes are expected to conform to the environmental regulations of the country of origin.

Cover photo © lussiya - Fotolia
Typeset by Datapage India Pvt Ltd
Printed and bound in Spain for Hodder Education, An Hachette UK Company, 338 Euston Road, London NW1 3BH

# Contents

# Guide to the book

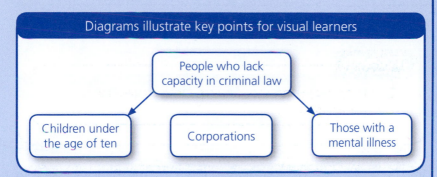

Diagrams illustrate key points for visual learners

People who lack capacity in criminal law

Children under the age of ten

Corporations

Those with a mental illness

Tick off what you have learnt and check you're on track

### Checkpoint - corporate manslaughter

| | |
|---|---|
| I can explain the effect of *C v DPP* (1995) on the doctrine of *doli incapax* | |
| I can suggest ways in which a Crown Court trial could be made more accessible to a child. | |

Provide you with potential real-life exam questions.
Answers are available on the accompanying website.

### Potential exam questions:

1) Assess the ways in which incapacitated defendants are dealt with in the criminal court system.

2) Examine the role of vicarious liability in criminal law.

3) Corporations can be indicted for criminal offences the same as individuals can.

# Guide to the website

There is useful additional material online to support your learning of tort law. Login at www.hodderplus.co.uk/law

## Model Answers

### Chapter 1

1. When the criminal law prosecutes and sentences criminals, its purpose is to:

   • incapacitate the criminal

   • punish the criminal

   • deter the criminal and the public

   • reform the criminal

   • educate the criminal and the public

   • affirm moral standards and restore justice in society.

## Useful links to websites to help you research further your studies in law

**www.parliament.uk**
The official Parliament website; use it to track all criminal bills currently before Parliament, explore the role of the House of Lords in law-making, and search for delegated legislation.

**www.legislation.gov.uk**
The official website for the Stationary Office; use it to search for newly enacted and revised legislation, draft legislation and statutory instruments for the United Kingdom, Scotland, Northern Ireland and Wales.

# Acknowledgments

The author would like to thank Lucy Winder, Sundus Pasha and Jasmin Naim at Hodder for their work on this project, and the reviewer for their comments on the manuscript.

# Preface

The Course Notes series is intended to provide students with useful notes, which are presented in a way that helps with visual learning.

The series is also interactive with:

- Workpoints for students to work through
- Research Points where students are invited to further their knowledge and understanding by referring to important source materials
- Checkpoints to see whether the reader has understood/ learned the key points on each topic
- Examination style questions at the end of each chapter.

There is also support available on the companion website where students can check their own answers to the examination-style questions against the suggested answers on the site, as well as interactive questions and useful links for research.

Jacqueline Martin

### Course Notes: Tort Law

Tort is an interesting subject for law students to study because of its relevance to everyday life. For example, if someone is injured in a car accident caused by another driver they will want to take legal action against the careless driver in the tort of negligence.

There are two main aims. Firstly, to provide a guide to the main legal principles, cases and statutes in tort and secondly to act as a revision aid.

The hope is that using the book will encourage students to develop their understanding of tort by further reading of some of the suggested articles and cases. This in turn should enable students to succeed in their examinations.

The purpose of this book can be compared to that of a walker's guide to the terrain ahead. It is a guide to help the student to navigate through that terrain rather than to be an exhaustive account of everything that the walker may encounter. It is not intended to replace the main textbooks on tort but to supplement them by providing help to check understanding and learning and to show approaches to answering questions.

Brendan Greene

# Table of cases

# Table of statutes and other instruments

## EU Legislation

### Conventions

### Directives

# Chapter 1
## Negligence: duty of care

## 1.1 Introduction

- The tort of negligence is the most important tort both in terms of academic study and in legal practice. Someone who suffers harm as a result of another's careless act may be able to claim in negligence. The law sets out certain requirements or elements which the claimant must prove for a successful claim.

- These questions must be considered:

1. Does the defendant owe a **duty** of care to the claimant?

2. Is the defendant in **breach** of that duty?

3. Is the defendant's breach of duty the cause of the **damage** to the claimant?

- If the answer to all three questions is 'yes', then the defendant is liable in negligence.

| Case: | |
|---|---|
| ***Donoghue v Stevenson* [1932]** | The claimant went into a café with a friend and the friend bought her a bottle of ginger beer which was in a dark brown bottle. The claimant drank some of the ginger beer but when she poured the rest into her glass it contained the remains of a snail and she was violently sick. She could not sue the café owner in contract because of the rule of privity but sued the manufacturer of the ginger beer. It was held that a manufacturer owes a duty of care to the consumer and here the manufacturer was negligent because he had allowed the snail to get into the bottle and there was no chance of an intermediate examination. |

- The modern law of negligence starts with one of the most famous of all legal cases which was decided by the House of Lords.

- Lord Atkin set out what became known as the **neighbour principle**.

*'You must take reasonable care to avoid acts or omissions which you can reasonably foresee would be likely to injure your neighbour. Who then in law is my neighbour? The answer seems to be persons who are so closely and directly affected by my act that I ought reasonably to have them in contemplation as being so affected when I am directing my mind to the act or omissions which are called in question'.*

## 1.2 The development of negligence

- In the period after *Donoghue v Stevenson* (1932) the tort of negligence gradually expanded to cover new duties which a defendant owed to a claimant.

| Case: | |
|---|---|
| **Home Office v Dorset Yacht Co [1970]** | Some borstal boys escaped from a camp, stole a yacht and collided with another yacht owned by the claimants, who sued the Home Office. The House of Lords held that the Home Office were liable for the negligence of the officers in omitting to supervise the boys. |

- Lord Reid said in relation to the *neighbour principle*, 'I think that the time has come when we can and should say that it ought to apply unless there is some justification or valid explanation for its exclusion'. Lord Reid was saying that in new situations the *neighbour principle* should apply unless there was a reason for it not to apply. This approach enabled the law of negligence to expand during the 1970s and 1980s. It became known as the modern approach of having a single general principle for the law of negligence.

> **Stage 1**
> Is there a relationship of proximity between the claimant and defendant such that the defendant ought to contemplate his careless act will cause harm to the claimant? If so then a second question is asked.

> **Stage 2**
> Are there any factors which would end the duty or restrict it? If there are no such factors then a duty is owed.

- In *Anns v London Borough of Merton* (1977) Lord Wilberforce refined Lord Reid's approach into a two-stage test.

- The House of Lords overruled *Anns* in *Murphy v Brentwood District Council* [1990].

- In *Caparo v Dickman* [1990] Lord Bridge said that the courts were moving away from looking for a single general principle. He cited Brennan J from an Australian case, *Sutherland Shire Council v Heyman* (1985):

*' … the law should develop novel categories of negligence incrementally and by analogy with established categories, rather than by a massive extension of a prima facie duty of care restrained only by indefinable considerations which ought to negative, or to reduce or limit the scope of the duty or the class of the person to whom it is owed'.*

- He went on to set out the three-stage test (see 1.3 below).

- The House of Lords was effectively restricting the development of negligence so that the law should gradually expand by using cases rather than by using a rather general legal principle.

### Workpoint

Can you explain how the law would develop incrementally?

Can you explain the opposite approach of having a general *prima facie* duty of care?

- **Point to note:** The two-stage test is not relevant when answering a problem question on negligence; the test to use is the three-stage test below.

- The two-stage test is only relevant when explaining the development of negligence.

## 1.3 Duty of care

### Definition

Duty of care: to establish this, the requirements of foreseeability, proximity and fair, just and reasonableness must be met.

- The first element of negligence to consider is the duty of care. The question is, does the defendant owe a duty of care to the claimant on the particular facts of the case?

- In *Caparo v Dickman* [1990] the House of Lords set out a three-stage test for determining whether a duty of care existed or not.

## 1.3.1 Duty of care – three-stage test

Foreseeability + Proximity + Fair, just & reasonableness = **Duty of care**

- This test is the universal test for determining whether a duty of care exists. All three stages have to be passed. The courts have moved away from trying to find a single general principle which can be used to determine whether a duty of care exists. The three stages are not mutually exclusive and there are relationships between all three factors, for example, if something is foreseeable, there is a higher chance of a relationship of proximity.

- This test is used for all types of harm whether it is physical harm, economic loss or psychiatric injury.

- There are certain established duties where it is not necessary to prove these three stages, for example:

  1. a manufacturer owes a duty of care to a consumer

  2. a road user owes a duty of care to other road users

  3. an employer owes a duty of care to employees

  4. a doctor owes a duty of care to patients.

### 1.3.1.1 Stage 1: Foreseeability

- The test of foreseeability is the question 'Could the reasonable man in the defendant's position have reasonably foreseen that the claimant would be injured if the defendant did the particular act?'

- This involves the concept of the **reasonable man** (or reasonable person) which brings in an *objective* test of someone's actions. It is whether the reasonable person would have foreseen the harm. This is in contrast to a *subjective test* of whether the individual defendant would have foreseen the harm. If a subjective test was applied then a defendant could simply say that they did not foresee the harm and they would not therefore owe a duty of care.

- Psychiatric harm (or nervous shock) is a special type of harm which is recognised in the law of negligence and damages may be claimed if certain conditions are met (see Chapter 5.4).

| Case: | |
|---|---|
| **Bourhill v Young [1942]** | The claimant, a pregnant Edinburgh fish seller, was getting off a tram when she heard an accident. The defendant, who was speeding on his motorbike, crashed into a car and was killed. The claimant was 15 metres away behind a tram and did not see the accident but later saw blood on the road. She suffered nervous shock and had a miscarriage. She sued for negligence. The court held that it was not reasonably foreseeable that someone so far away would suffer shock and no duty of care was owed. |

## 1.3.1.2 Stage 2: Proximity

- The word 'proximity' means nearness or closeness. The legal term is **proximity of relationship** which is derived from Lord Atkin's neighbour principle in *Donoghue v Stevenson* (1932).

- The claimant needs to prove proximity of relationship and this may be done by proving physical closeness, closeness of relationship or a policy reason. It may even be a combination of some of these factors.

- If the defendant is **physically close** to the claimant it is more likely there will be proximity. For example, if the defendant is practising golf swings with a golf club a few metres away from another person, they will have a proximity of relationship with that person.

- **Closeness of relationship** may be shown by some previous contact between the claimant and defendant or by the nature of the relationship between them.

| Case: | |
|---|---|
| **Watson v British Boxing Board of Control [2000]** | During a boxing match, Watson suffered brain damage. Although the British Boxing Board of Control (BBBofC) did not organise boxing matches, it was responsible for regulating them. This included rules on safety and medical facilities. If a suitable doctor had been at the ringside then Watson's brain damage would have been prevented. The BBBofC was responsible for the rules and this created a relationship of proximity with boxers who relied on appropriate rules being in place. The BBBofC was negligent. |

- **Policy** may be another reason for saying that there is or is not a closeness of relationship. Generally the courts make decisions by using **legal principles** and precedents. Sometimes courts may make decisions for **policy reasons**, which means a non-legal reason for making a decision. It covers a wide range of matters. Policy reasons may be used to create a duty or to stop a duty arising.

- Policy reasons include:

    1. the floodgates argument, that making the defendant liable would open the flood gates to claims;

    2. that claims would be paid from public funds and the defendant should not therefore be liable;

    3. that the defendant has insurance and can pay so should be liable.

| Case: | |
|---|---|
| **Hill v Chief Constable of West Yorkshire [1988]** | The mother of the last victim of the Yorkshire Ripper sued the police for negligence, on behalf of her daughter's estate, claiming that the police should have arrested him earlier. Was there proximity between the police and the daughter? She was one of many women at risk and there was no proximity of relationship with the police. The Court also took into account policy reasons that if the police were made liable they would be worried about people suing them. This would lead to defensive policing and the police diverting resources to deal with claims. The police were not liable. |

## 1.3.1.3 Stage 3: Fair, just and reasonable

- Even if there is **foreseeability** and **proximity,** a court may say that there is no duty of care because in all the circumstances it would not be fair, just and reasonable to impose a duty on the defendant.

- This stage also allows policy factors to be taken into account, for example, in *Hill v Chief Constable of Yorkshire Police* [1988] it would not be just and reasonable to impose liability on the police because of the large number of potential victims.

| Case: | |
|---|---|
| **Vowles v Evans [2003]** | During an amateur rugby match the prop forward of one team was injured and was replaced by an inexperienced player. As a result the scrum kept collapsing and the claimant, who played for the opposing team, was injured. It was part of the amateur referee's role to make the decision on substitutes but he had left it to the team captain. Did the referee owe a duty of care to the players? The players should be able to rely on the referee carrying out his job carefully and it was fair, just and reasonable that he should be liable. |

## Workpoint

Ann owns a clothes shop in London. One night in the summer of 2011 her shop window was smashed by rioters and lots of clothes were stolen from the shop. Ann lived above the shop and called the police but they did not arrive until two hours later.

Becky lives in a house which is situated 20 metres from a road but at a point where there is a sharp bend. Colin is driving his 40-tonne truck along the road but is travelling too fast, skids off the road at the bend and the lorry crashes into Becky's house.

Carla is playing hockey in an amateur match. Doris, who is playing for the other team, swings her hockey stick to hit the ball but misses and strikes Carla on the leg, breaking it.

Explain whether a duty of care in negligence can be established by:

(a) Ann;

(b) Becky;

(c) Carla.

## Research Point

Read 'Policy and the function of duty' in M. Jones, *Textbook on Torts* (8th edn, Oxford: Oxford University Press, 2002, pp 41–49). In the light of the extract consider how the courts use policy in making decisions. What arguments can you identify both in favour of using policy and against?

## Research Point

Look up the case of *Smith v Chief Constable of Sussex Police* [2008] UKHL 50 and *X v Bedfordshire County Council* [1995] 2 AC and identify the policy reasons used in each case for reaching the decisions.

## Checkpoint – duty of care

| Task | Done |
|------|------|
| I can state the three requirements to establish a duty of care | |
| I can explain the test of foreseeability | |
| I understand what policy reasons are in decisions of the courts | |
| I can explain the decision in *Hill v Chief Constable of West Yorkshire Police* (1988) | |

• **Point to note:** The three-stage test for proving a **duty of care** must be distinguished from the three-stage test to prove **liability in negligence**.

Foreseeability + Proximity + Fair, just & reasonableness = **Duty**

Duty + Breach + Damage = **Liability in negligence**

## Potential exam question

Critically assess how the courts use policy in determining whether or not a duty of care exists in negligence.

Please read Chapters 1, 2, 3 and 4, and some of the suggested reading and any articles on policy, before attempting this question.

# Chapter 2
# Negligence: breach of duty

## 2.1 The standard of the reasonable person

- Once a duty of care has been established, the next question is whether the defendant is in breach of this duty.

- In answering this question the courts look at the standard of the defendant's conduct. This is judged by using the standard of the **reasonable person.** This is an *objective* standard which is imposed on the defendant. It does not take *subjective* factors into account, for example, the physical strength of the defendant. If the defendant does not reach the standard of the reasonable person then the defendant is negligent. The law is using a hypothetical person to set the standard.

- Note that traditionally, the cases have referred to the standard of the **reasonable man** but it is more appropriate in modern times to talk about the **reasonable person.** Judges have often referred to the reasonable man as 'the man on the Clapham omnibus'.

- The standard was set out by Baron Alderson in *Blyth v Birmingham Waterworks* [1856]:

*'Negligence is the omission to do something which a reasonable man ... would do or doing something which a prudent and reasonable man would not do'.*

- The standard was explained by Lord Macmillan in *Glasgow Corporation v Muir* [1943]: 'It eliminates the personal equation and is independent of the idiosyncrasies of the particular person whose conduct is in question'.

| Case: | |
|---|---|
| ***Glasgow Corporation v Muir* [1943]** | Mrs A was manageress of the Corporation tea rooms and she allowed a private party to use the tea rooms. Two members of the party were carrying a tea urn along a narrow passage, when one of them let go of the handle and some children were scalded by hot tea. Was Mrs A negligent in allowing them to carry the urn? It was held that the reasonable man would not have closed the passage while the tea urn was being moved and Mrs A was not negligent. |

• The reasonable person is not the perfect person, nor the average person. It is someone who will usually act in a reasonable way. It is the judge in the individual case who determines this standard.

# 2.2 Qualifications on the objective standard

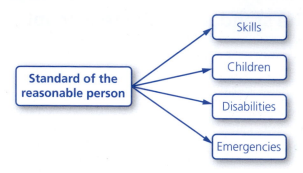

## 2.2.1 Skills

• If a person has a particular skill they are not judged by the standard of the **reasonable person** who does not have that skill.

> **Definition**
>
> The *Bolam* test: a person with a particular skill must reach the standard of an experienced competent person with that skill.

| Case: | |
|---|---|
| ***Bolam v Frien Hospital Management Committee* [1957]** | B suffered from depression and agreed to electro-convulsive therapy. He was not given relaxant drugs or physical restraints and fell and broke his pelvis. There were different views amongst doctors whether to give relaxant drugs or restrain the patient, or neither. It was held that the defendant doctor had acted in accordance with a competent body of medical opinion and was not negligent. |

• McNair J said, 'A man need not possess the highest expert skill; it is well established law that it is sufficient if he exercises the ordinary skill of an ordinary competent man exercising that particular art'.

- In *Bolitho v City and Hackney Health Authority* [1997] the House of Lords put a qualification on the *Bolam* test. They said that before accepting a medical opinion as 'responsible' a court had to be satisfied that doctors had considered the risks and benefits of the proposed treatment and had reached a 'defensible' conclusion.

- The effect of this decision is that a court will not simply accept what a responsible body of doctors says but can consider if their opinion has a logical basis.

- If someone carries out a skilled task but lacks the skill or experience to reach the *Bolam* standard, they will be in breach of their duty of care.

| Case: | |
|---|---|
| **Nettleship v Weston [1971]** | The defendant asked her friend, the claimant, to teach her to drive. On the third lesson the defendant suddenly drove on to the pavement, hit a lamppost and the claimant was injured. The defendant was liable in negligence because they did not reach the standard of the competent and experienced driver. |

- The effect of the above decision is that the defendant cannot escape liability because they lack skill and experience. It may seem that the law imposes too high a standard on a learner, in any field, but the standard can be reached through proper supervision.

## 2.2.2 Children

- The standard of care applied to children is the standard of a reasonable child of the same age.

| Case: | |
|---|---|
| **Mullin v Richards [1998]** | Two 15-year-old schoolgirls were friends. They were having a sword fight with plastic rulers during a lesson when a ruler snapped and a piece of plastic went in the claimant's eye and she went blind. The test of foreseeability was whether a reasonable child of the same age would foresee the risk. There was no evidence that such rulers broke easily, nor that playing games with them had been banned. The defendant had not been negligent. |

The Court applied this standard from *Mullin* more recently.

| Case: | |
|---|---|
| ***Orchard v Lee*** **[2009]** | A 13-year-old schoolboy was playing tag in the playground at lunch time and ran into a supervisor and injured her. The Court of Appeal said that the boy was playing the game in the normal way and not breaking any rules. For a child to be negligent they had to act with a 'very high degree' of carelessness. The boy was not negligent. |

## 2.2.3 Disabilities

• If a claimant has a disability and the defendant knows or should know this, then the defendant owes them a higher standard of care. In *Haley v London Electricity Board* [1964] a blind man fell into a trench in the street. A pick axe handle had been put across the front of the trench. This would have been a sufficient warning for someone with normal sight but in this case was negligent.

• If a defendant has a disability but does not realise, this must be taken into account in deciding if the defendant is in breach of their duty of care.

| Case: | |
|---|---|
| ***Mansfield v Weetabix*** **[1998]** | The defendant's lorry driver suffered from a condition which caused a hypoglycaemic state which affected his brain. He did not know about his condition and did not realise it affected his driving. He crashed into the claimant's shop. The Court of Appeal held that the standard of care was that of a competent driver who did not know they had a condition which impaired their ability to drive. The defendant was not negligent. Otherwise the defendant would have been liable but would not have been at fault. |

• The above decision is in contrast to the following earlier case.

| Case: | |
|---|---|
| **Roberts v Ramsbottom [1980]** | The defendant, a 73-year-old driver, collided with the claimant's parked car. The defendant argued that he was not negligent because he had had a stroke 20 minutes before the accident, but during that 20 minutes he had also been in two other accidents. The court said that he continued to drive even though he should have realised that he was ill and he was therefore negligent. |

## 2.2.4 Emergencies

- If the defendant is acting in an emergency this is taken into account in deciding what standard they have to reach, e.g. if someone stops to give first aid at a road accident, the fact it is an emergency and they will not have medical resources will be taken into account.

### Workpoint

Ali, aged 20, is playing football for an amateur team and carries out a high tackle and injures an opponent.

Ben, aged 12, is rollerskating in the park with his friend Chris. He collides with Chris and injures him.

Donna, aged 18, is washing up some dishes at home and drops a glass, which shatters and cuts her mother Eve.

Farouk, a doctor, witnesses a road accident and goes to help the injured driver but makes the injuries worse.

Identify what standard Ali, Ben, Donna and Farouk must reach.

# 2.3 Determining the standard of care

In deciding if the defendant is in breach of the duty of care, the courts take a number of factors into consideration. The factors set out below are not exclusive and the courts can also take other relevant factors into account.

The factors have to be considered not only individually but in relation to each other. For example, if it is easy to avoid an injury and the act has little social value, that would suggest a breach of duty. In *The Wagon Mound (No 2)* [1967] the court took into account that discharging oil into Sydney harbour was not a benefit to anyone and could easily have been prevented.

### 2.3.1 Likelihood of injury

- The more likely that an injury is to occur, the higher the standard expected of the defendant.

| Case: | |
|---|---|
| **Bolton v Stone [1951]** | Miss Stone was standing in the street outside a cricket ground when she was hit by a cricket ball. The cricket ball had been hit nearly 100 metres over a three-metre high fence. This had happened only six times in 30 years. It was held that it was foreseeable that someone outside the ground would be hit, but the likelihood of injury was extremely small and the defendants were not negligent. |

### 2.3.2 Seriousness of injury

- If there is a risk of more serious injury then a higher duty of care is expected from the defendant.

| Case: | |
|---|---|
| **Paris v Stepney Borough Council [1951]** | The claimant only had one good eye and worked in the defendant's garage. The defendant knew about his eye. He was working under a vehicle when a splinter of metal flew into his good eye and blinded him. He had not been given goggles which was the normal practice. The House of Lords held that even though the risk of injury was small and his disability did not increase that risk, it did increase the risk of serious injury i.e. the claimant goes blind. Therefore the defendant was liable. |

## 2.3.3 Cost of avoiding the injury

- What measures must the defendant take to avoid the risks of harm? The more likely the risk has of happening or the more serious the consequences could be, the greater the duty on the defendant to take steps to avoid the injury. The defendant only has to reach the standard of the reasonable person in taking those steps.

| Case: | |
|---|---|
| *Latimer v AEC* [1953] | A heavy rainstorm caused a river to burst its banks and flood the defendant's factory. The water mixed with oil and made the factory floor slippery. The defendant put down sawdust but some of the floor was untreated. The claimant fell on the untreated part and was injured. He argued that the defendants should have closed the factory. The House of Lords said that it was a matter of balancing the risk against the measures needed to eliminate it. Only one person had been injured and there was no need to close the whole factory. The defendant was not negligent. |

## 2.3.4 Social value of the defendant's action

- If the defendant is doing an act which is a benefit to society, the courts will balance this against the risk the defendant is taking.

| Case: | |
|---|---|
| *Watt v Herts County Council* [1954] | After a road accident someone was trapped under a car. A heavy jack was needed to lift the car. The fire brigade used an unsuitable lorry to transport the jack and it slipped and injured the claimant fire officer. He sued for negligence. The Court of Appeal heard that if the fire brigade had waited ten minutes, a suitable lorry would have been available. It was held that the defendants did owe a duty of care to the claimant but the defendants were trying to save a life and had fulfilled their duty. |

- Denning LJ said of this case:

*'If this accident had occurred in a commercial enterprise without any emergency there could be no doubt that the servant would succeed. But the commercial end to make a profit is very different from the human end to save life or limb'.*

- Note that the reference to 'servant' means employee.

## Research Point

Look up *Watt v Herts CC* [1954] 1 WLR 835 and read the judgment of Denning LJ.

Explain what he said about balancing the risk.

To what extent do you agree with Denning LJ about fire engines etc. stopping at red lights?

- The Compensation Act 2006 s1 provides that a court, in considering whether the defendant should have taken certain steps to meet a standard of care, may take into account whether a requirement to take those steps might prevent a desirable activity or discourage people from doing things in connection with a desirable activity.

## Checkpoint – breach of duty

| Task | Done |
| --- | --- |
| I can explain the standard of the reasonable person | |
| I can name and define the standard applied to someone with a skill | |
| I can explain the effect of a disability of the claimant or defendant on the standard | |
| I can state four important factors the courts use to determine the standard of care | |

## Research Point

Look up the following article: Morgan, J. (2009), Policy reasoning in tort law: the courts, the Law Commission and the Critics, *LQR*, 125 (Apr).

# 2.4 *Res ipsa loquitur*

- *Res ipsa loquitur* means 'the thing speaks for itself'. This maxim applies in situations where it is clear that the harm could not have happened unless the defendant had been negligent.

| Case: | |
|---|---|
| **Scott v London & St Katherine Docks Co (1865)** | The claimant was injured when some bags of sugar, being lowered by crane in the defendant's warehouse, fell on him. The defendant could not explain the accident but the court said that the bags of sugar would not fall without negligence and the defendant was liable. |

## 2.4.1 Requirements for *res ipsa loquitur*

Requirements for *res ipsa loquitur*

- Injury would not happen without negligence
- No explanation for the injury
- Defendant has control of thing causing injury

### 2.4.1.1 The injury would not normally happen without negligence

- This was seen in *Scott v London and St Katherine Dock Co.* (1865). It is also obvious in cases where things are left inside patients during operations.

| Case: | |
|---|---|
| **Mahon v Osborne [1939]** | The claimant had an operation on their abdomen. Later it was discovered that a swab (a cotton wool pad) had been left in their body. The defendant surgeon was unable to explain this. It was held that *res ipsa loquitur* applied and he was liable in negligence. |

### 2.4.1.2 There is no explanation for the accident

- If there is evidence of how the accident happened then it is up to the claimant to establish negligence. If there is no evidence of how the accident happened then *res ipsa loquitur* will apply.

| Case: | |
|---|---|
| **Barkway v South Wales Transport [1950]** | The claimant's husband, a passenger on a bus, was killed when the bus ran off the road and crashed. This would not normally happen. But there was evidence that a tyre had burst and *res ipsa loquitur* did not apply. It was up to the claimant to prove negligence which they did by showing the system of tyre inspection was negligent. |

### 2.4.1.3 The defendant has control of the instrument causing the harm

- The following two cases illustrate this requirement.

| Case: | |
|---|---|
| **Gee v Metropolitan Railway Co. (1873)** | The claimant leaned against the door of a train and fell out. The train had recently left the station. It was held that the defendant had control of the train and the door and *res ipsa loquitur* applied. |

| Case: | |
|---|---|
| **Easson v London and North Eastern Railway Co. [1944]** | The claimant, aged 4, fell out of the door of a train. The train had travelled seven miles from the station. It was held that the defendant did not have control of the door, as any passenger going along the train corridor could have opened the door. *Res ipsa loquitur* did not apply. |

## 2.4.2 The effect of *res ipsa loquitur*

- In a civil case the burden of proof is on the claimant. There has been debate whether the effect of the maxim is to reverse the burden of proof, so that it is up to the defendant to prove they were not negligent. In *Ng Chun Pui v Lee Chuen Tat* [1988] the Privy Council said that *res ipsa loquitur* does not reverse the burden of proof. The burden of proof is on the claimant throughout the case.

- If the claimant claims *res ipsa loquitur* and the defendant shows that there is some explanation for the accident then it is up to the claimant to prove that the defendant was negligent.

## Potential exam question

Amira is a newly qualified nurse and obtained her first job at the Bee NHS Hospital. One night Amira went out with her friends to celebrate obtaining her new job. The next morning she was tired when she arrived at work. She was giving medication to Chris, a patient, but mixed him up with the patient in the next bed and gave Chris the wrong medication. As a result Chris became violently ill and was admitted to the intensive care unit for two days.

Daljit, a 14-year-old boy, was playing in a football match at school. He jumped up to head the ball in a challenge with Eric but elbowed Eric in the face and broke Eric's nose. .

Fred owned a garage. He received a phone call from Gina informing him that she was driving along, collided with a bus and her car was badly damaged. Fred was rushing to the scene of the accident in his large recovery truck, drove through a red traffic light and collided with Harry who had just cycled through a traffic light on green. Harry was badly injured.

Advise (i) Amira, (ii) Daljit and (iii) Fred of their legal position in the above situations.

# Chapter 3

# Negligence: causation

## 3.1 Factual causation

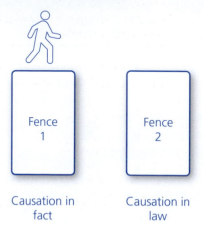

Fence 1 — Causation in fact

Fence 2 — Causation in law

- The third requirement to prove negligence is that the defendant's breach of duty **caused** the damage to the claimant. It is up to the claimant to prove this on a balance of probabilities.

- To establish that the defendant's act caused the damage there are two stages to be satisfied:

  1. factual causation, and if this is proved

  2. legal causation.

- Factual causation means that the defendant's act was the factual cause of the claimant's damage.

- The test used to prove this is known as the 'but for' test.

The question is: would the claimant have suffered damage *but for* (or *were it not* for) the defendant's act?

- The answer to this question must be 'no' to satisfy the test. If the answer is no, that the claimant would not have suffered the damage, then logically the defendant's act caused the damage.

- The test was applied in the next case:

| Case: | |
|---|---|
| **Barnett v Chelsea & Kensington HMC [1969]** | Three night watchmen had been drinking tea and started vomiting. They went to the defendant's hospital and the nurse telephoned the duty doctor who said that they should go home and see their own GPs. A few hours later one of them died from arsenic poisoning. The doctor owed a duty to the men and had broken that duty by not examining them. Did the breach cause the death? The evidence was that even if he had been admitted he would have died anyway. Therefore the doctor's negligence did not cause the death and the hospital was not liable. |

- The above case is an example of when the result of the 'but for' test is clear. There are more complex factual situations when this test is not suitable.

- **Problem Situations**
  - Multiple causes
  - Consecutive causes
  - Loss of a chance

## 3.1.1 Multiple causes

- There are a number of situations when the test does not work. One example is if there are two or more causes. A famous example of this is set out below.

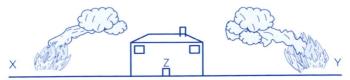

X          Z          Y

- For example, X carelessly starts a fire and at the same time, Y carelessly starts a fire. The two fires spread and at the same time burn down Z's house. If the 'but for' test is used:

1. Would Z's house have burned down but for X's careless act? The answer is 'yes' because the fire started by Y would have burned down the house. Therefore X is not liable.

2. Would Z's house have burned down but for Y's careless act? The answer is 'yes' because the fire started by X would have burned the house down. Therefore Y is not liable.

- The result is that neither X nor Y is liable in negligence. This is unjust and the law has developed other tests. One of those tests is the test of 'material contribution'.

| Case: | |
| --- | --- |
| **Bonnington Castings v Wardlaw [1956]** | The claimant developed a lung disease from dust while working in the defendant's factory. Some of the dust was from pneumatic hammers and it was impossible to prevent this dust. Some of the dust was from grinders which had not been maintained properly and this dust could have been prevented. It was not possible to tell which dust caused the disease. The court asked whether the dust from the grinders had made a 'material contribution' to the disease and concluded that it had. Therefore the defendant was negligent. The court said that anything other than a minimal amount would make a material contribution. |

- The same test can also be used in cases where the defendant's act **materially increased** the risk of harm.

| Case: | |
| --- | --- |
| **McGhee v National Coal Board [1972]** | The claimant worked in a brickworks and developed dermatitis from the brick dust. The dust he was exposed to while working could not be prevented but he had to cycle home covered in dust because no showers were provided. C had to prove that the dermatitis was caused by the dust on him on the way home. This was impossible to prove using the 'but for' test. The court held that the defendant had 'materially increased' the risk of dermatitis by not providing showers and was therefore negligent. |

- A distinction has been made by the courts between cases where there was only one factor that causes the harm and cases where there are a number of separate factors. In McGhee there was only brick dust but in the next case there were five separate possible causes.

| Case: | |
|---|---|
| **Wilsher v Essex Area Health Authority [1988]** | The claimant was born prematurely, given too much oxygen and went blind. The blindness could have been caused by too much oxygen or any one of four other conditions. The claimant also suffered from the four conditions. The court said that if there were a number of different causes of the harm the claimant had to prove, on a balance of probabilities, that it was too much oxygen rather than one of the other causes. It was impossible to prove which caused the blindness and the claim failed. |

## 3.1.1.1 Multiple tortfeasors

- A problem with causation also arises if instead of two or more causes there are two or more people who could have caused the harm (or one person and some other cause). In these circumstances the courts also use the test of 'material contribution'.

| Case: | |
|---|---|
| **Fairchild v Glenhaven Funeral Services Ltd [2002]** | While working for a number of employers the claimants were exposed to asbestos dust and as a result developed mesothelioma. It was possible that the disease could be caused by a single fibre of asbestos. It was impossible for the claimants to prove which employer was responsible. The 'but for' test could not provide an answer. The court held that by exposing the claimants to the risk of mesothelioma this was a material contribution to contracting that disease. All the employers were liable. |

- The liability of the employers was **joint and several**. This means that the claimant can sue all the employers or just sue one for all the damage caused.

- In the above case the courts are trying to balance two opposing claims. Should they:

  1. impose liability on an employer who has not been shown to have caused the harm, or

2. not compensate an employee who has suffered harm but cannot prove which employer is responsible for it.

- It can be argued that this is really a matter of policy as to which factor takes precedence in trying to achieve justice.

- The above rule of joint and several liability was amended in the following case.

| Case: | |
| --- | --- |
| **Barker v Corus UK Ltd [2006]** | The claimant had three jobs which had all exposed him to asbestos and as a result he contracted mesothelioma and died. He worked for an employer which became insolvent, for the defendant and for himself. In the House of Lords Lord Hoffman said that the justification for joint and several liability is that if you caused harm there was no reason why your liability should be reduced because someone else also caused the same harm. If liability is imposed, as in this case, because you may have caused harm, the same justification does not apply. If more than one person is responsible, liability should be divided according to the probability that one or other caused the harm. The effect is that the defendant is only liable for the proportion of risk he exposed the claimant to and this is several liability. Therefore the defendant was not liable for the insolvent employer's share. Further the claimant was found to be 20% contributory negligent for the period he worked for himself. |

- The Compensation Act 2006 s3 reversed the effect of *Barker*. Under s3(1) if a person has negligently exposed someone to asbestos and as a result the victim has contracted **mesothelioma** and it is not possible to tell if that exposure or some other exposure caused the victim to become ill, a person is liable in tort. Under s3(2) if others have also exposed the victim to asbestos then liability is joint and several.

- **Point to note:** The Compensation Act 2006 only applies to mesothelioma.

**Research Point**

Look up the case of *Sienkiewicz v Grief (UK) Ltd* [2011] UKSC 10. The High Court said that the defendants increased the risk of exposure to asbestos by 18% and dismissed the claim because the claimant could not prove the case on a balance of probabilities.

Explain the decision of the Supreme Court and the reasons why they reached that decision.

## 3.1.2 Consecutive causes

• What is the legal position if after the original negligent act there is a second negligent act causing harm to the claimant?

| Case: | |
|---|---|
| ***Baker v Willoughby* [1970]** | While driving his car the defendant negligently knocked down the claimant, injuring the claimant's leg. The claimant worked in a scrap yard. Three years after the accident during a robbery at work the claimant was shot in the same leg and as a result it had to be amputated. Did the effect of the second injury blot out the effect of the first injury so that the robbers were liable for loss after the shooting? The House of Lords said that a person is not compensated for the injury but for the loss that he suffers. After the first injury the claimant was not able to lead a full life or earn as much as he did before the accident. The second injury did not affect these matters. The defendant was liable for the full extent of the injuries for the remainder of the claimant's life. |

• The position is different if the claimant contracts an unrelated illness after the original negligent act.

| Case: |  |
|---|---|
| *Jobling v Associated Dairies* **[1982]** | In 1973 the claimant slipped over at work due to the defendant's negligence and injured his back. His earning power was reduced by 50%. In 1976 before the case came to trial the claimant developed an unrelated disease of the spine which left him unable to work. The High Court awarded damages for the remainder of his life. The House of Lords applied the 'but for' test, which failed. They also said that the disease was one of the misfortunes of life, which courts took into account anyway in awarding damages. The aim of damages in tort was to put the claimant in the same position as before the tort. If damages were given for the time after 1976 the claimant would be in a better position than if he had not been injured. The defendants were only liable up to the time he developed the disease. |

## 3.1.3 Loss of a chance

- In some situations the claimant is arguing that due to the defendant's negligence the claimant has **lost the chance**, for example, of making a full recovery from illness. The claimant must prove their case on a balance of probabilities, that is, at least 51%.

| Case: |  |
|---|---|
| *Hotson v East Berkshire Health Authority* **[1987]** | The claimant, a 13-year-old boy, fell out of a tree. He went to hospital but was sent home. Five days later it was discovered that he had broken his hip and he developed a deformity of the hip. If he had been correctly diagnosed and treated when he first went to hospital he would have had a 25% chance of making a full recovery. He was awarded 25% compensation by the High Court. The House of Lords said that the claimant had to prove, on a balance of probability, that the delay caused the deformity. He was unable to do so because he only had a 25% chance of recovery. Therefore he was not entitled to any compensation. |

- The House of Lords left open the question whether damages could ever be claimed for loss of a chance. The same approach was taken in the next case.

| Case: | |
|---|---|
| **Gregg v Scott** [2002] | The defendant doctor wrongly diagnosed the claimant as having a harmless lump under his arm. A year later it was correctly diagnosed as malignant. The claimant argued that if he had originally been diagnosed correctly, he would have had a 42% chance of recovering but now only had a 25% chance. It was held that he was unable to prove on a balance of probabilities that he would have survived. |

## Checkpoint – causation in fact

| Task | Done |
|---|---|
| I can explain the 'but for' test | |
| I can identify circumstances when the courts use the test of 'material contribution' | |
| I can distinguish between *Baker v Willoughby* (1970) and *Jobling v Associated Dairies* (1982) | |
| I can explain what s3 Compensation Act 2006 provides | |
| I can explain what was decided in *Gregg v Scott* (2002) and why the claimant lost | |

# 3.2 Legal causation

- Even when it is established that the defendant's negligent act has factually caused the harm it still remains to be established whether the defendant should be liable as a matter of law. This involves the **test of remoteness**: if the damage is too remote from the defendant's act the defendant will not be liable.

- The original test for deciding if damage was too remote was the 'direct consequences' test which meant that the defendant was liable for all consequences directly linked to the negligent act (*Re Polemis* [1921]). This test has effectively been replaced by the test of 'reasonable foreseeability' which was established in the following case.

| Case: |
|---|

| **The Wagon Mound (No 1) [1961]** | The defendants carelessly spilled oil from their tanker into Sydney harbour. The claimants were carrying out welding at their wharf about 200 metres away and all welding was stopped when oil was seen along the wharf. The claimants were told it was safe to continue welding as it was believed that the oil would not burn on water. Molten metal from the welding fell on to some cotton rag soaked in oil in the water and a fire started which damaged the wharf. The Privy Council held that it was not reasonably foreseeable that the wharf would catch fire as a result of the defendant's negligent act and the defendant was not liable. |

## 3.2.1 Type of damage

* The defendant will only be liable if the type (or kind) of damage was reasonably foreseeable. In *The Wagon Mound (No 1)* [1961] it was foreseeable that the oil would foul the wharf but not that it would cause damage by fire.

* The defendant does not have to foresee the full extent of the damage.

| Case: |
|---|

| **Hughes v Lord Advocate [1963]** | Some Post Office employees were working down a manhole. They put a tent over the hole and four paraffin lamps around it and went off for tea. Two boys aged 8 and 10 went up to the hole and started playing with a lamp. The claimant knocked the lamp into the hole, paraffin vapourised, was ignited by the flame and caused an explosion. The claimant was badly burned. The defendant argued that this chain of events was very unusual and could not be foreseen so they were not liable. The House of Lords said that it was foreseeable that children might play with the lamps and that paraffin might spill and cause a fire. Whether the burning is caused by liquid paraffin or paraffin which has vapourised, they both cause burns. The claimant had suffered a foreseeable type of harm, burning. The defendant was liable in negligence. |

- The kind of damage was damage by burning. The House of Lords said that the distinction between 'burning' and 'explosion' was too fine a distinction. A contrasting decision was seen in the next case.

| Case: | |
|---|---|
| **Doughty v Turner Manufacturing [1964]** | The defendant had a bath of sodium cyanide heated to 800 degrees Centigrade. The lid was made of asbestos. It was carelessly knocked into the bath and it reacted with the sodium cyanide causing an explosion. The claimant was standing nearby and was burned. The Court of Appeal said that the type of harm that was foreseeable was injury by splashing if the lid was knocked into the bath. But here there was a chemical reaction which could not be foreseen and the defendant was not liable. |

- *Doughty* takes a narrow view of what was foreseeable. If the type of harm was injury by 'burning' the defendant would have been liable. The courts now seem to be taking a wider view of the foreseeable harm. In *Jolley v Sutton LBC* [1998] the House of Lords identified the harm as some physical injury from meddling with the boat (see Chapter 10, 10.3.1).

## Research Point

Look up *Hughes v Lord Advocate* (1963) (HL) and read the judgment of Lord Guest and his statement about paraffin vapour and liquid paraffin. The result seems to be that if the claimant suffers a foreseeable kind of damage they can then recover compensation no matter how it is caused.

Explain whether this is too favourable to the claimant.

## Workpoint

Aimi suffers a nose bleed and goes to the Wessex NHS Hospital. Bella, a nurse, tells her to see her family doctor and sends her away. Aimi catches a bus to go to the doctors' but loses more blood, faints and has to be taken to hospital by ambulance for treatment.

*Continued overleaf*

Chris lived in a mining village and worked in Don's coalmine for over 30 years. He has now developed silicosis of the lungs. It is unclear whether the disease has been caused by dust from the mine or dust in the air in the village.

Erica went to see Fred, her family doctor, about a small mole on her skin. Fred said it was harmless. Six months later Erica discovered that the mole was cancerous and she has been told that she has one year to live. If it had been correctly diagnosed when she first went to see Fred, Erica would have had a 50% chance of making a full recovery.

Explain in each case what test Aimi, Chris and Erica would use to establish causation and whether they can do so.

## 3.3 New intervening acts

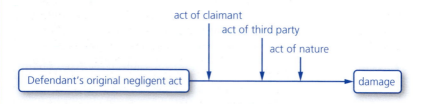

- After the defendant's negligent act there may be another act or event which also causes harm to the claimant. This second act may be sufficient to break the 'chain of causation' between the defendant's act and the claimant's harm.

- If this is established, the second act is known as a **new intervening act** (*novus actus interveniens*). The result is that the defendant is not liable for negligence.

- What is enough to break the chain of causation has to be determined in each case taking into account if the later act was foreseeable and the degree of negligence. There are three situations to consider.

## 3.3.1 Act of the claimant

- If the claimant does an act after the defendant's negligent act which overrides the defendant's act, the result is that the claimant is liable for the harm. The court asks the question – was the claimant's act unreasonable in all the circumstances? But see *Spencer* below.

| Case: | |
|---|---|
| *McKew v Holland* [1969] | Due to the defendant employer's negligence the claimant suffered an injury to his left leg, which resulted sometimes in a loss of control of the leg. Soon after the injury he was going down some steep stairs with no handrail, whilst holding his grand-daughter's hand. His leg gave way and to avoid falling on his head he jumped. He landed and broke his right ankle. The House of Lords said that although jumping was reasonable, going down the stairs in the first place was unreasonable and it was a new intervening act. The defendant was not liable for the broken ankle. |

- If the claimant's act does not amount to a new intervening act it may be sufficient to be **contributory negligence** (see Chapter 14, 14.3).

| Case: | |
|---|---|
| *Corr v IBC Vehicles* [2007] | Due to his employer's negligence the claimant suffered serious head injuries and depression. Six years after the accident he committed suicide. The House of Lords said that it was foreseeable the claimant would suffer depression as a result of the accident. Although committing suicide was the claimant's own act it was the result of the depression and was not a new intervening act. The defendant was liable. |

- Although the claimant's act of committing suicide is unreasonable, the depression was caused by the defendant's negligence.

| Case: | |
|---|---|
| *Spencer v Wincanton Holdings Ltd* [2009] | Due to the defendant's negligence the claimant suffered a leg injury and had to have one leg amputated. He was given an artificial leg but could not use it for driving and he used two sticks when walking short distances. Over three years after the accident he went to a petrol station to fill up his car. He was not wearing his artificial leg or using sticks and tripped over and was injured. But for the defendant's negligent act he would not have suffered the later injuries. It was held that the defendant was liable for the later injuries. The court deducted one third for contributory negligence. |

- The usual approach taken is to determine whether the claimant's act was unreasonable. In *Spencer* the court said that because the meaning of 'unreasonable' was so wide-ranging it was better to use a test of 'fairness'. On the facts of *Spencer* it was fair to hold the defendant liable.

## 3.3.2 Act of a third party

• After the defendant's negligent act a *third party* may commit a second act which causes harm to the claimant. The question is whether this second act is enough to break the chain of causation. In deciding this question the courts take a number of factors into account including whether the third party's act was foreseeable and whether it was reasonable in all the circumstances.

| Case: | |
|---|---|
| ***Scott v Shepherd* (1773)** | The defendant threw a firework into a market place and it landed near T's stall. T picked it up and threw it away. It landed near the claimant and exploded, injuring him. Who should be liable, the defendant or T? The court said that T's act of throwing the firework away was not a new intervening act, as T was simply protecting himself. The defendant was held liable for battery. |

D ────────▶ T

C

| Case: | |
|---|---|
| ***Knightley v Johns and others* [1982]** | Johns negligently caused an accident in a one-way tunnel. The police inspector who arrived at the scene forgot to close the tunnel in accordance with police regulations. He then sent Knightley, a police motorcyclist, down the tunnel against the traffic, to close it. Knightley collided with Cotton who was driving in the right direction and Knightley was badly injured. He sued Johns, the Chief Constable, Cotton and the inspector for negligence. The court said that Johns's negligence was too remote from the second accident and he was not liable; the Chief Constable was not negligent because his position was covered by the regulations; Cotton was not negligent because he could not expect to meet someone going the wrong way; but by not closing the tunnel and sending Knightley the wrong way the inspector had committed a new intervening act and was liable. |

- In the above case the court accepted that in a crisis mistakes can be made. In deciding if the harm caused is too remote from the original accident, decisions have to be made on the basis of common sense.

- If, as a result of the defendant's negligence, someone tries to rescue the claimant and causes further harm will the rescuer's act be a new intervening act? An act of rescue is very unlikely to break the chain of causation.

| Case: | |
|---|---|
| *The Oropesa* [1943] | Due to the negligence of the captain of the ship *The Oropesa* it collided with another ship and damaged it. The captain of that ship sent crew in a lifeboat to consult the captain of *The Oropesa* about saving his damaged ship. The lifeboat capsized in heavy seas and some of the crew drowned. It was held that given the dangerous position he was in, the captain's decision was not a new intervening act. The captain of *The Oropesa* remained liable for negligence. |

- If the claimant needs medical treatment as a result of the defendant's negligence and that treatment is negligent, will it break the chain of causation? It is foreseeable that if the claimant is injured they will need medical treatment and it is also foreseeable that such treatment could be given negligently. It is unlikely to break the chain of causation unless it is grossly negligent.

## 3.3.3 Act of nature

- The situation may arise that after the defendant's negligent act further harm is caused to the claimant or the claimant's property by an act of nature e.g. a storm, lightning, etc. Does such a natural event break the chain of causation?

| Case: | |
|---|---|
| *Carslogie Steamship Co v Royal Norwegian Government* [1952] | The claimant's ship was damaged in a collision caused by the defendant. The ship sailed to the United States for repairs but on the journey suffered further damage in a storm. The claimant argued that but for the defendant's negligence, the ship would not have had to sail to the United States and would not have suffered the storm damage. The House of Lords held that the storm broke the chain of causation and the defendant was not liable for the further damage. |

• This can equally apply where the claimant suffers injury, see *Jobling v Associated Dairies* [1982].

# 3.4 The eggshell skull rule

• If the type of harm is foreseeable, the eggshell skull rule says that if the claimant, due to some sensitivity, suffers more harm than a normal person, the defendant is liable for that harm.

• Examples could be:

  • Thin ('eggshell') skull

  • Weak heart

  • Haemophiliac

  • Shabby millionaire

  • Nervous condition.

• The rule means that the defendant must take their victim as they find them.

• If the normal test of foreseeability was applied, the harm to the claimant would not be foreseeable and the defendant would not be liable.

| Case: | |
|---|---|
| *Smith v Leech Brain* **[1961]** | The claim was brought by the employee's wife. Due to the negligence of his employer, a drop of molten metal caused a small burn on the employee's lip. The burn caused a dormant cancer to develop and the employee died. The defendant argued that the death was not foreseeable as a result of the burn. It was held that the defendant could foresee the type of harm, a burn, and was therefore liable for his death. |

| Case: | |
|---|---|
| *Robinson v Post Office* **[1974]** | The claimant slipped on an oily ladder at work and cut his leg. He was given an anti-tetanus injection by a doctor but was allergic to the vaccine and suffered brain damage. An allergy test would not have revealed the allergy. The defendants argued that they were only liable for the injury to the leg. The Court of Appeal said that it was reasonably foreseeable that if the claimant was cut he would need medical treatment. The defendant was liable for the consequences of that treatment even though he could not foresee it could be serious. |

## Checkpoint – causation in law and new intervening acts

| Task | Done |
|---|---|
| I can explain the test of reasonable foreseeability to establish causation in law | |
| I can understand the distinction between the decisions in *Hughes v Lord Advocate* (1963) and *Doughty v Turner Manufacturing* (1964) | |
| I can explain what is meant by a new intervening act and its significance | |
| I can identify three types of new intervening acts and give case examples | |
| I can explain the eggshell skull rule | |

## Research Point

Please read the following article: O'Doherty, S. (2009), Personal Injury: Causation: a floating concept, 159 *NLJ* 809.

1) Explain the test of causation used if the scientific evidence cannot prove that the defendant's negligence caused the harm but just increased the risk.

2) Explain the test of causation used in *Fairchild* [2003].

3) Explain the arguments (i) that the deceased did break the chain of causation in *Corr v IBC* [2008] and (ii) that he did not break the chain of causation.

## Potential exam question

Alan was crossing the road at a zebra crossing when he was knocked down by a car driven by Bob. Bob was late for an appointment and was speeding. As a result of the accident Alan's right leg was so badly damaged it had to be amputated. Although he was fitted with an artificial leg he sometimes lost control of it.

A year after the accident Alan was driving his car when he lost control of his right leg and was unable to brake at a bend. The car went off the road and through a fence into Celia's garden. Celia was mowing her lawn and the car collided with her and she fell to the ground breaking her arm. Alan's windscreen shattered in the accident and his face was cut by flying glass.

The collision also caused a can of petrol, which Celia was using for her lawnmower, to be thrown into the air. The can of petrol landed in Don's garden 50 metres away and exploded. Don was sunbathing in the garden and was badly burned in the explosion.

Advise (i) Alan, (ii) Celia and (iii) Don of any claims they may make in negligence.

# Chapter 4

## Negligence: omissions, third parties, rescuers, public bodies and the emergency services

## 4.1 Omissions

- The general rule in negligence is that someone is **not** liable for an omission.

- Although in *Donoghue v Stevenson* (1932) Lord Atkin spoke of liability for 'acts and omissions' he meant omissions in the course of conduct. For example, if a pilot is landing a plane but omits to brake and crashes into the airport fence the pilot will be liable in negligence.

- But a person is not liable for an omission which is not related to a course of conduct. For example, if you see someone fall off a pier into the sea and drown you are not liable in negligence for failing to save them.

### 4.1.1 Exceptions to general rule that there is no liability for omissions

- The law creates exceptions to the general rule if there is a particular relationship between the parties.

### 4.1.1.1 The defendant assumes responsibility for the claimant

| Case: | |
|---|---|
| **Barrett v Ministry of Defence [1995]** | An off-duty pilot at an RAF base in Norway drank himself into a coma. He was found and taken to his room where he later choked on his vomit and died. The Court of Appeal said that there was no duty to stop an adult drinking alcohol but once the defendant found the pilot in a coma they assumed responsibility for him. They were negligent for not calling for medical help. However, the dead pilot was found to be 25% contributorily negligent. |

In *Mitchell v Glasgow City Council* [2009] (see 4.2 below), there was no assumption of responsibility by the council to protect the claimant.

### 4.1.1.2 The defendant has a position of responsibility

• Some examples are:

  • a parent has a duty to rescue their child

  • a doctor has a duty to help their patient

  • a captain has a duty to rescue a passenger

  • a lifeguard has a duty to rescue a swimmer

  • the police have a duty to help a prisoner.

### 4.1.1.3 The defendant creates the danger

• If the defendant creates the danger they are under a duty to act to help the claimant.

| Case: | |
|---|---|
| **Capital and Counties v Hampshire CC [1997]** | The fire brigade do not owe a duty of care to individual houseowners. But if the fire brigade created the danger or made it worse, they could be liable. The defendants attended a fire in a factory. A fire officer ordered the sprinkler system to be turned off and as a result the factory burned down. The defendants were held liable in negligence. |

# 4.2 Liability for the acts of third parties

- In tort one person is not normally liable for harm to a second person caused by a third person (or third party). For example, A is not liable for harm to B which is caused by C.

| Case: | |
|---|---|
| ***Perl v London Borough of Camden*** **[1984]** | The defendant council owned a block of flats and rented one to the claimant for his business. The flat next door to it was empty and there was no lock on the front door. Thieves went into the empty flat, knocked a hole in the wall and burgled the claimant's business. The Court of Appeal said that the risk of burglary was foreseeable because there was no lock on the front door. But the defendant council had no control over the burglars and were not liable for their actions. |

| Case: | |
|---|---|
| ***Mitchell v Glasgow City Council*** **[2009]** | The claimant family and a third party rented houses from the defendant. The third party had made violent threats to the claimants on several occasions. The defendant had a meeting with the third party and told him that he would be evicted. The third party then murdered the father of the family. The family argued that the defendants knew about the threats and should have warned the family about the meeting. The House of Lords said that although harm was foreseeable, there was not a relationship of proximity and it was not fair, just and reasonable to impose a duty on the defendants to warn the family. |

## 4.2.1 Exceptions to the rule of no liability for acts of third parties

| proximity of C and D | proximity of D and TP | D creates danger |
|---|---|---|

## 4.2.1.1 Relationship of proximity between claimant and defendant

- Each situation needs to be considered to establish if there is sufficient proximity. A contractual relationship can create proximity.

| Case: | |
|---|---|
| **Stansbie v Troman [1948]** | The defendant decorator was left alone to decorate the claimant's house. He promised to lock the door if he went out but forgot to do so. The claimant was burgled. It was held that there was proximity between the claimant and defendant as there was a contract between them. The defendant was liable. |

- Recently it has been established that there is proximity between a nightclub and a guest.

| Case: | |
|---|---|
| **Everett and Harrison v Comojo Ltd [2011]** | E & H went to d's nightclub. B, a regular visitor to the club, saw one of them pat K, a waitress, on the bottom. B said he would make them apologise. Later in the evening B's driver, C, arrived. K was afraid that trouble would start and told the manager. Shortly afterwards C stabbed both E and H with a knife. E & H claimed that the defendants were negligent for not searching guests and that K should have told the head of security not the manager. The Court of Appeal said: (i) an assault by a third party was foreseeable given alcohol was available; (ii) there was proximity between the club and guests, as clubs wished to make money from them; (iii) it was fair, just and reasonable to impose a duty on the management provided the scope of the duty was appropriate. But B had never caused trouble and even if K had told security, the violence happened so quickly they could not have stopped it. Therefore the defendants were not liable for the actions of the third party. |

## Research Point

Look up the following article: Butler,S, and Urquuhart, C. (2011), Negligence: Serving up trouble, 161 *NLJ* 236.

Explain how the three requirements for a duty of care apply in *Everett*.

To what extent do you agree with the decision in that case?

Consider whether a simple precaution, like searching all guests on entry, may have prevented the stabbing. If so, what effect would this have on the decision?

## 4.2.1.2 Relationship of proximity between the defendant and the third party

• If the defendant has control over the third party this may lead to a relationship of proximity if it is also foreseeable that the claimant will suffer harm. This was established in the following case.

| Case: | |
|---|---|
| **Home Office v Dorset Yacht Co [1970]** | Borstal boys were camping on Brownsea Island under the supervision of three prison officers. The officers went to bed leaving the boys unsupervised. The boys stole a yacht and crashed into the claimant's yacht. The Home Office argued it could not be liable for the acts of third parties. It was held by the House of Lords that it was foreseeable that if they escaped the boys would take a yacht. The officers had ignored instructions by leaving the boys unsupervised, they were responsible for controlling the boys and the Home Office was negligent. |

## 4.2.1.3 The defendant creates the danger

• If the defendant negligently creates the danger and it is foreseeable that a third party will use that danger to injure the claimant, the defendant will be liable.

| Case: | |
|---|---|
| **Haynes v Harwood [1935]** | The defendant left a horse-drawn van unattended in a busy street. A child threw a stone at the horse, which bolted. The claimant police officer was injured when he tried to stop the horse. The court said that it was foreseeable that someone would try and stop the horse in the circumstances and the defendant was liable for the act of the child. |

- The courts have to determine what can be regarded as a special danger leading to liability and what would be seen as a normal danger for which there would be no liability.

| Case: | |
|---|---|
| **Topp v London Country Bus Ltd [1993]** | The defendant left a minibus unlocked with the keys in the ignition at a bus stop near a pub. It was normal practice to do this between shifts but the next driver failed to turn up. A third party stole the minibus and knocked down and killed the claimant's wife. The Court of Appeal held that leaving the minibus in this condition did not create a special danger and the defendant was not liable for the act of the third party. |

- It seems that there is a fine line between these two cases: the unattended horse is dangerous but the minibus with the keys in it is not.

## Checkpoint – liability for acts of third parties

| Task | Done |
|---|---|
| I can explain the general rule on liability for acts of third parties | |
| I can describe the three exceptions to that rule | |
| I can explain the decision in *Everett v Comojo Ltd* (2011) | |
| I can distinguish *Haynes v Harwood* (1935) from *Topp v London Country Bus Ltd* (1993) | |

# 4.3 Rescuers

- A person is not liable in negligence for an omission. Consequently, there is no legal duty to rescue someone in danger.

## 4.3.1 Duty owed by rescuers

- The courts are slow to find rescuers negligent or contributory negligent. In *Tolley v Carr* [2010] C's negligent driving resulted in her car stopping sideways across the outside lane of a motorway, creating a danger to other road users. T checked to see the road was clear but was injured trying to move the car. C admitted liability for negligence and it was held that T had acted reasonably in going to the rescue and was not contributory negligent.

## 4.3.2 Duty owed to rescuers

- If a defendant puts someone or some property in danger and a rescuer goes to help and is injured, is the defendant liable to the rescuer? If it is foreseeable that someone will go to the rescue the defendant owes a separate duty of care to the rescuer. A duty is owed to both amateur and professional rescuers.

- In *Haynes v Harwood* [1935] the defendant put others in danger by leaving a horse-drawn van untethered in a busy street. He was found liable to the police officer who was injured stopping the runaway horse.

- In *Chadwick v British Railways Board* [1967] a duty was owed to a rescuer who lived near a railway line, went to help after a train crash and suffered psychiatric harm.

- In *Ogwo v Taylor* [1988] a duty was owed to a fire officer who was injured putting out a fire in the defendant's house.

## 4.3.3 Defendant puts themselves in danger

- If the defendant puts themselves in danger, the defendant will owe a duty of care to a rescuer as long as the rescue is not foolhardy.

| Case: | |
|---|---|
| ***Baker v Hopkins*** **[1959]** | The defendant's employees used a petrol engine pump to pump water out of a well. The employees were overcome by carbon monoxide fumes from the pump. The claimant doctor went down the well to help them but he was also overcome by the fumes. All three died. The doctor knew of the danger but was trying to save lives. It was held by the Court of Appeal that trying to rescue the employees was not foolhardy and the doctor had not consented to the risk. His estate was entitled to compensation. |

• Does a rescuer assume responsibility by helping? There is no clear answer from the cases, see *Capital Counties v Hampshire CC* [1997] and *Kent v Griffiths* [2001].

## Research Point

Look up Fulbrook, J. (2011), Case Comment: Personal Injury: contributory negligence – rescuers, (*Tolley v Carr* (2010)), *JPIL*.

Link your understanding of rescuers with the defences of consent and contributory negligence (see Chapter 14) and particularly consider the case of *Crossley v Rawlinson* [1981] 3 All ER 674.

## Workpoint

A is walking along the bank of a canal and sees B trip and fall into the canal. A carries on walking.

C, a life guard at a swimming pool, is walking along the bank of a canal and sees F trip and fall into the canal. C carries on walking.

E is walking along the bank of a canal and sees F trip and fall into the canal. E jumps in to help F but in doing so kicks F on the head and injures him.

G, a school teacher, is escorting a group of 15-year-old pupils on a geography field trip to the seaside. H, a pupil, picks up a pebble from the beach and throws it at I, another pupil, causing an injury to I.

Advise A, C, E and G of their liability, if any, in negligence.

# 4.4 Public bodies

• The question of whether a public body can be made liable in negligence at common law is a difficult one.

• There are many sound policy reasons why a public body should not be made liable:

1. Paying compensation will divert resources from providing services.

2. It may lead to defensive practices to avoid being found liable.

3. There may be alternative ways to obtain a remedy e.g. judicial review of a decision of a public body.

• In many cases a public body will be acting under statutory powers. This raises the important question whether the statute imposes a **duty to act** (must) or merely gives a **power to act** (may).

- The courts have distinguished between **policy matters**, which involve the authority deciding how resources are allocated which involves the exercise of discretion, and **operational matters** which are decisions about how tasks or services are performed.

- It has been argued that there could not be liability in negligence for **policy matters** but there could be liability for **operational matters**.

However, in practice it has been difficult to make this distinction.

- The general position taken by the courts is that public bodies are **not** liable in negligence.

| Case: | |
|---|---|
| ***X v Bedfordshire County Council* [1995]** | This involved five claims in negligence against the local authority involving failure to take children into care with the result they suffered abuse and failure to provide for the special educational needs of children. The House of Lords said that the tests of foreseeability and proximity were met. However, it was not fair, just and reasonable to impose a duty. The statutory system to prevent abuse involved many other public agencies and to make one liable would be unjust. To impose a duty on all of them would make it impossible to determine which one was liable. The defendants were not liable. |

| Case: | |
|---|---|
| ***Stovin v Wise* [1996]** | The defendant drove out of a side road and collided with the claimant motorcyclist, injuring him. The defendant said that she could not see the claimant because of a bank of earth at the junction. The local authority knew that the junction was dangerous and had the power to remove the earth but had not done so. The question was whether the local authority could be liable in negligence for this omission to exercise its statutory power. The House of Lords said that two conditions must be met: (i) it must have been irrational for the authority not to exercise the power; and (ii) there had to be 'exceptional grounds' for compensation to be paid. Taking no action was not irrational as there was no duty to act; as there was no liability for breach of statutory duty to maintain the highway, no duty of care arose from not doing so. The local authority was not liable for failure to act. |

- This decision confirmed that it is difficult to sue a public authority for a failure to exercise its powers.
- The courts later showed that the strict rule against liability could be relaxed.

| Case: | |
| --- | --- |
| **W v Essex County Council [2000]** | The claimant parents wished to foster a child and told the defendants that they did not want anyone who abused children. The defendants placed a 15-year-old boy with the claimants without mentioning that he had abused children. The boy abused their children and they suffered psychiatric harm. The Court of Appeal rejected the claim because as a matter of policy the defendants should not be liable in negligence as it would interfere with their statutory duty to foster children. The House of Lords said that the claimants had an arguable case. The case was later settled out of court. |

| Case: | |
| --- | --- |
| **Connor v Surrey County Council [2010]** | The claimant head teacher was wrongly criticised and subjected to intimidating behaviour by some of the school governors. She asked the defendant council for support, as they had power to remove the governors and appoint an interim board. As a result of the intimidation she suffered psychiatric harm. The defendant argued that its powers were discretionary and they did not have to act. The Court of Appeal said that the defendant owed the claimant a duty of care as her employer, which was a separate duty to any duty arising from the exercise of a statutory power. The defendant had breached this duty of care as an employer by the failure to exercise its statutory discretion. |

- This decision shows that public bodies need to be aware that in exercising their statutory powers they may owe a duty in negligence.

The government reduce funding to local authorities. Consequently a local authority cuts the funding for school buses. This means that some children have to walk home along country roads with no pavements. John, aged 14, is knocked down by a car while walking along a country road on the way home from school and injured.

Explain whether or not the local authority is liable in negligence to John.

# 4.5 The police and other emergency services

## 4.5.1 The police

- A negligence claim against the police may be made in respect of an **operational matter** or a **policy matter**.

- An **operational matter** is about how the police carry out their day to day work and the police may be liable in negligence. For example, you are walking along the pavement and are knocked down by a police car. You may sue the police for negligence.

- A **policy matter** is about the allocation of resources.

| Case: | |
|---|---|
| ***Rigby v Chief Constable of Northamptonshire* [1985]** | A burglar broke into the claimant's gun shop and started firing guns. The police fired a CS gas canister into the shop which started a fire. The police knew the risk of fire but did not have firefighting equipment. The court found that if the equipment had been available less damage would have been done. The defendants were negligent. |

- The courts have refused claims in negligence in such cases. The leading case is *Hill v Chief Constable of West Yorkshire* [1988] where the House of Lords said that the police were not liable in negligence mainly because it would lead to defensive policing and would divert resources to dealing with such claims. No duty of care was owed to individual members of the public.

- The courts have followed the *Hill* principle and this was confirmed by the House of Lords in the following two cases which were heard together.

| Case: | |
|---|---|
| **Smith v Chief Constable of Sussex [2008]** | S told the police that he had received phone calls and text messages from J, his former partner, threatening to kill him. The police did not take any action. Shortly afterwards J attacked S with a hammer and badly injured him. S sued the police for negligence. It was held that the police were not liable even though information had been given about a known third party. The police were immune from liability to individuals in the interests of the wider public. |

| Case: | |
|---|---|
| **Van Colle v Chief Constable of Hertfordshire Police [2008]** | VC was a witness in a prosecution against B for a minor theft. Before the trial VC received threatening phone calls from B. The property of some witnesses was damaged although this was not traced to B. No protection was provided for VC. Just before the trial B shot VC dead and B was convicted of murder. VC's parents claimed a breach of VC's right to life under Article 2 of the European Convention on Human Rights. It was argued that because the police made VC give evidence this put him at risk. It was held that in order to succeed there had to be a 'real and immediate' risk to the life of an identified person. B had no record of violence and on the facts there was no real and immediate risk to VC. The claim failed. |

### Workpoint

Look up McIvor, C. (2010) Getting defensive about police negligence: the *Hill* principle, the Human Rights Act 1998 and the House of Lords, *CLJ*.

To what extent do you agree with the author that the immunity enjoyed by the police under the *Hill* principle should be reversed?

## 4.5.2 The fire brigade

- Like the police the fire brigade owe no duty of care in negligence to individuals. There is no duty in negligence to attend a fire after a 999 call. However, if on attending a fire, the defendants make the position worse the fire brigade will be liable. In *Capital and Counties v Hampshire Fire Brigade* [1997] the fire brigade attended a fire and the fire officer in charge turned off the sprinkler system, with the result that the building burned down. The court held that the fire brigade were liable in negligence because they had made the position worse; it was an act no reasonable fire officer would do.

## 4.5.3 The ambulance service

- The courts have decided that the ambulance service do owe a duty of care in negligence to individuals in certain circumstances.

| Case: | |
|---|---|
| ***Kent v Griffiths* [2000]** | The pregnant claimant had an asthma attack and her doctor went to see her. The doctor called an ambulance which took 40 minutes to travel six miles. While waiting the claimant stopped breathing and as a result lost her baby. The Court of Appeal said that once a call was accepted this created a duty of care. The service provided was more like the NHS which owed a general duty to the public, rather than like the police or the fire brigade. The defendants had breached their individual duty to the claimant. |

- The duty arose when the call was accepted. The situation would be different if no ambulances were available and a caller was told to wait, as no duty would then be owed.

## Checkpoint – public bodies and the emergency services

| Task | Done |
|---|---|
| I can distinguish operational and policy matters | |
| I understand the principle behind *X v Beds CC* (1995) | |

## Checkpoint – continued

| | |
|---|---|
| I can explain the decision in *Connor v Surrey CC* (2010) | |
| I can describe the *Hill* principle | |
| I can explain why *Van Colle (2008)* failed under Art 2 | |
| I can explain the position of the fire and ambulance services in negligence | |

## Potential exam question

Ally owns a boat which is permanently moored on a river. Ally operates a night club which is based on the boat. One evening Bob and Cath went to the night club and spent the evening drinking. Dave, a known troublemaker, was also in the night club that evening. Dave started an argument with Bob and swore at him. Later in the evening Dave deliberately started a fight with Bob and stabbed him with a knife causing a serious injury. Bob was taken to hospital.

Even though Cath had consumed several alcoholic drinks she decided to drive to the hospital in her car. On the way, due to her alcoholic condition, Cath lost control of the car and collided with Eve, who was crossing the road on a pedestrian crossing. As a result of the collision Eve broke her leg.

Fred was walking along the river bank at midnight and saw George swimming in the river. George appeared to be struggling in the strong current and shouted for help. Fred jumped in to rescue him but in doing so Fred hit a submerged rock and broke his arm. George managed to swim to the bank of the river.

Advise (i) Ally, (ii) Cath and (iii) George of their liability, if any, in negligence.

# Chapter 5

# Negligence: economic loss, negligent mis-statements and psychiatric injury

## 5.1 Introduction

- There are certain areas in negligence to which special rules apply. These include economic loss, negligent mis-statements and psychiatric harm. The law has developed special rules for these types of loss to restrict the claims which may be brought. The distinction made between economic loss caused by acts and economic loss caused by statements has caused difficulties and is not based on logic.

## 5.2 Economic loss

> **Definition**
>
> Economic loss: financial loss which does not arise from injury, death or damage to property.

- For example, Ali drives negligently on the motorway and causes an accident and as a result a traffic jam develops. Beth is delayed in the traffic jam, is late for work and loses two hours' pay. Beth's loss is **pure economic loss**.

- The general rule in tort is that you **cannot** claim for pure economic loss.

- The courts have taken policy reasons into account in making decisions on economic loss. Economic loss is seen as different to personal injury or property damage arising from a negligent act. In those cases the number of people affected will be limited e.g. causing a road accident will only affect a relatively small number of people. In contrast, causing a power cut to a town will lead to many suffering economic loss and could open the floodgates to claims.

- You can claim for economic loss which is a consequence of injury or damage to property. This is known as **consequential economic loss**.

- For example, Ali negligently crashed into Beth's car and Beth was injured and as a consequence had to stay off work for a week and lost a week's pay. The loss of pay would be consequential economic loss resulting from her injury and she could claim for her pay, in addition to damages for her injury.

| Case: | |
|---|---|
| ***Spartan Steel Ltd v Martin Ltd*** **[1973]** | The claimants were steel makers. The defendants negligently cut the electricity cable to the claimant's factory. The claimants claimed for: (i) damage caused to metal in the furnace which solidified and had to be thrown away; (ii) loss of profit on that metal; and (iii) loss of profit on further metal that could have been processed while the factory was closed. It was held that they could claim for (i), which was physical damage, and (ii), which was consequential economic loss, but not (iii), which was pure economic loss. |

- If someone bought goods or property which had a defect that would be pure economic loss and they could not claim in tort. However, the courts took a different view in the next case.

| Case: | |
|---|---|
| ***Anns v Merton LBC*** **[1978]** | The claimant bought a flat. Some time later cracks appeared in the walls and it was found this was caused by defective foundations. The claimant sued the defendant local authority for negligently inspecting the foundations. It was held by the House of Lords that the cracks were physical damage to the building and the defendants were liable to pay compensation. |

- This decision went against the principle that damage to the property itself could not be claimed in tort.

| Case: | |
|---|---|
| ***Junior Books v Veitchi* [1983]** | The claimants entered a contract with the main contractor to build a factory and told them to employ the defendants, who were specialists, to lay the floor. The floor was laid negligently and the factory had to close while the floor was re-laid. The claimant sued in negligence for the cost of re-laying the floor and loss of profit while the factory was closed. The court said that the defendants knew the claimants relied on their skill and it was foreseeable the claimant would suffer loss if the defendants acted negligently. There was close proximity between them and so the defendants were liable. |

*profit*

- These cases showed that the tort of negligence was expanding and covering new types of claim, which previously would only have been allowed if there was a contract in place.

- The courts later began to restrict the law of negligence. In *Murphy v Brentwood District Council* [1990] the House of Lords overruled *Anns*.

| Case: | |
|---|---|
| ***Murphy v Brentwood District Council* [1990]** | The claimant's house was built on a concrete raft. The design of the raft had been negligently approved by the defendant council. As a result the walls began to crack. The claimant sold the house for much less than it should have been worth and sued the defendant for the difference in value. The House of Lords said that there was no damage to other property, only to the house itself. This was economic loss and the claim failed. |

## Workpoint

Read *Spartan Steel v Martin & Co* [1973] QB 27 and in particular the judgment of Lord Denning MR.

Identify the five considerations he took into account and explain whether you would agree with his reasons.

## 5.2.1 Defective property

• Can a claim be made for defective property?

| Case: | |
|---|---|
| **Muirhead v Industrial Tank Specialties [1985]** | The claimant fish merchant planned to buy lobsters when they were cheap, keep them in tanks of sea water and sell them at Christmas for a high price. He bought pumps for the tanks from a supplier but the pumps did not work properly because the motors were the wrong voltage for the UK. All the lobsters died. The supplier went bankrupt and the claimant sued the manufacturer of the pumps in negligence. He claimed: (i) cost of lobsters and loss of profit on them; (ii) money spent trying to fix the pumps; (iii) loss of profit on the business. It was held that he could claim for (i) as the lobsters were 'other property' and the profit was consequential loss; but not (ii) and (iii) which were pure economic loss. The claimant could not prove that he had relied on the manufacturer. |

• The result is that claims for defective property can only be made in contract.

## 5.2.2 Exceptions to the rule that no claim can be made for economic loss

### 5.2.2.1 *Junior Books Ltd v Veitchi* [1983]

• This case remains valid but has been regarded by the courts as confined to its own facts i.e. a very close relationship between the parties which is very close to a contract.

### 5.2.2.2 The wills cases

• A number of cases which involve solicitors and wills has provided another exception (see Section 5.3.6 below). These involve a solicitor preparing a will negligently or failing to prepare a will.

## Checkpoint – economic loss

| Task | Done |
|---|---|
| I can define economic loss | |
| I can explain the decision in *Spartan Steel v Martin* (1973) | |

| Checkpoint – continued | |
|---|---|
| I can explain the effect of the decision in *Murphy v Brentwood District Council* (1990) | |
| I understand the legal position on claims for defective property | |
| I can state two exceptions to the general rule on claims for economic loss | |

# 5.3 Negligent mis-statements

- It is important to distinguish between a **negligent act** and a **negligent statement.**

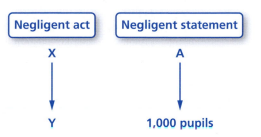

| Negligent act | Negligent statement |
|---|---|
| X | A |
| ↓ | ↓ |
| Y | 1,000 pupils |

**Definition**

Negligent act: effect is generally quite limited e.g. driving negligently and crashing into another car.

Negligent statement: can have a widespread effect e.g. a school nurse telling 1,000 pupils in a school assembly that if they burn their hand they should put it in hot water.

- Because of the fear of opening the floodgates to claims the law has developed special rules dealing with negligent statements.

- In most circumstances the claim is for economic loss so allowing such a claim is an exception to the general rule that no claims can be made in tort for economic loss.

- The original rule was that no claim could be made in tort for a negligent statement. A claim could only be made for a fraudulent statement (see *Derry v Peek* (1889)(HL)).

```
           letter
NPB  ◄───────────────────  D
 │                          │
 │                          │
 ▼                          │
 C      ........contract........  E Ltd
```

| Case: | |
|---|---|
| **Hedley Byrne v Heller [1964]** | The claimant advertising agents wished to enter a contract with E Ltd. The claimants asked NPB, their own bank, to find out about E Ltd. NPB contacted the defendants, E Ltd's bank, who sent a letter stating that E Ltd were good for 'ordinary business engagements'. The letter also said that the advice was given 'without responsibility'. NPB told this to the claimants, who then entered a contract with E Ltd. E Ltd later went into liquidation and the claimants lost £17,000. At the time the defendants gave the reference, E Ltd were heavily overdrawn. The claimants sued for the negligent mis-statement. It was held that, on the facts, the defendant was not liable because of the exemption clause. However, the court set out the principles for liability. |

- The House of Lords set out the three requirements for a duty to arise in respect of a negligent mis-statement. These requirements overlap to some extent.

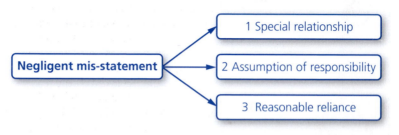

## 5.3.1 Special relationship

- This will arise if the person giving the information knows that the other party is relying on the information.

- It will normally arise in **business situations**. The person giving the advice does not have to be someone who gives advice as part of their job, like an accountant or a solicitor. It is sufficient if the advice is given in the course of a business. All the circumstances have to be taken into account.

| Case: | |
|---|---|
| **Patchett v Swimming Pool Association [2009]** | The defendants, a trade association, had a website with a list of swimming pool installers. The claimant chose one from the list and entered a contract with them. The installer became insolvent. The claimant sued the defendant for negligent mis-statement. The installer was not a full member of the association. The website advised customers to make independent enquiries and obtain an information pack from the defendants. The claimant had not asked for a pack. It was held that there was not sufficient proximity for a special relationship and the defendant was not liable. |

- In contrast to business situations a statement made on a **social occasion**, for example, giving someone advice at a party on what shares to buy will not lead to liability. This rule must now be seen in the light of the following decision.

| Case: | |
|---|---|
| **Chaudry v Prabhakar [1989]** | The claimant asked the defendant, a friend with some knowledge of cars, to find a second hand car for her but not one that had been in an accident. The defendant obtained a car with a repaired bonnet which had been in an accident. It was unroadworthy and the claimant sued. The defendant conceded that he owed a duty and the case was decided on breach. The Court of Appeal held by a 2/1 majority that even though the defendant was not paid, the claimant was relying on the defendant's skill. He owed a duty of care, had breached that duty and was liable. |

• May LJ dissenting said that imposing a duty in social situations was hazardous for relationships.

## 5.3.2 Voluntary assumption of responsibility

• Although many cases have spoken about a **voluntary assumption of responsibility** by the defendant, the courts have had difficulty in determining when this arises.

| Case: | |
|---|---|
| **Merrett v Babb [2001]** | The defendant surveyor carelessly valued a house for a building society. His employer gave the valuation to the claimant who bought the house in reliance on the survey. The employer went into liquidation. The claimant sued the defendant surveyor personally for negligence. It was held that the defendant should have realised that the buyer would rely on his skill. He had signed the valuation report and therefore assumed responsibility for it. He was liable even though he had no insurance! |

## 5.3.3 Reasonable reliance

• The claimant must show:

  • that they **relied** on the statement by the defendant, and

  • that it was **reasonable** to rely on the defendant.

• In *Caparo v Dickman* [1990] the claimant relied on accounts prepared by the defendants for a company AGM (Annual General Meeting), in order to buy shares in the company. The accounts were inaccurate and the claimant lost money. However, it was not reasonable to rely on the accounts which had been produced to protect shareholders as a group.

## 5.3.4 Third parties relying on the statement

• If the statement is made to one party but a third party relies on it, can the third party claim under *Hedley Byrne v Heller*?

| Case: | |
|---|---|
| **Goodwill v British Pregnancy Advisory Service [1996]** | M, a married man, had a vasectomy carried out by the defendants, who told him he did not need to use contraception. Three years later he started a relationship with the claimant and told her about his vasectomy. Some time later the vasectomy reversed naturally and the claimant became pregnant by M and had a baby. She sued the defendant for the cost of bringing up the baby. The court said that the claimant had to show: (i) the defendant knew the advice would be acted on by the claimant without independent enquiry; and (ii) the claimant had acted on the advice to her detriment. The defendant did not know about the claimant and could not know their advice would be given to her. The defendant was not liable. |

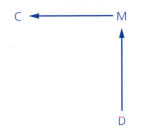

$$C \longleftarrow M$$
$$\uparrow$$
$$D$$

**Workpoint**

Anna, a solicitor, advised Bianca, a client, to buy shares in a particular pharmaceutical company. Anna met Cleo at a party and advised her to buy shares in a new online music company. A week later Cleo told her friend Donna to buy some shares in the same music company.

Eric, a mechanic, advised Fred, a work colleague, to buy shares in X Bank.

All the above shares fell 90% in value within a few weeks of being purchased.

Identify if Bianca, Cleo, Donna and Fred would have claims for negligent mis-statement.

## 5.3.5 Exclusion clauses

- The defendant may seek to rely on an exclusion clause or disclaimer. Whether this is successful will depend on whether it is used between two businesses or between a business and a consumer.

| Case: | |
|---|---|
| **Smith v Bush [1989]** | A house buyer applied to a building society for a mortgage. The building society instructed a surveyor to carry out a survey but also advised the buyer to have their own independent survey. The surveyor carried out the survey negligently and later a chimney collapsed. The surveyor's report contained an exemption clause. It was held that the surveyor would know that the buyer would rely on the report even though it was prepared for the building society. The buyer paid a fee for the surveyor. The surveyor owed a duty to the buyer. The exemption clause was unreasonable under s2 Unfair Contract Terms Act 1977. The surveyor was liable in negligence. |

- In *Smith v Bush* [1989] the buyer was purchasing a modest house. If the buyer is a Premiership footballer buying a very expensive house the footballer would be expected to obtain their own surveyor's report.

- In *Scullion v Bank of Scotland plc* [2011] the Court of Appeal has limited the application of *Smith v Bush*.

| Case: | |
|---|---|
| **Scullion v Bank of Scotland (t/a Colleys) [2011]** | The claimant was purchasing a buy-to-let flat and the valuation was carried out by Colleys for the mortgagee (lender). The claimant bought after seeing the valuation but this was negligent and the flat was sold for £80,000 less than the purchase price. The claimant sued the valuers. The Court of Appeal said that the claimant had to establish foreseeability, proximity and fair, just and reasonableness. It was accepted that the valuer knew it was likely the claimant would see the report, rely on it and had paid a fee to the mortgagee for the valuation. The court took into account that with buy-to-let properties: (i) it was a commercial transaction and purchasers could afford their own valuation; (ii) in *Smith v Bush* valuers knew 90% of buyers of homes relied on the valuation but this was not the case here; (iii) the purchaser is interested in the rental value which is a tricky matter and the valuer would expect a buyer to obtain their own report; and (iv) the valuer knows the mortgagee relies on the capital value so the loan can be repaid but the purchaser is not likely to rely on this valuation. In all the circumstances Colleys owed no duty of care to the claimant. |

# 5.3.6 The wills cases

| Case: | |
|---|---|
| **Ross v Caunters** **[1980]** | The claimant's husband witnessed a will in which the claimant was a beneficiary. The solicitor did not tell the testator that the gift would fail. The claimant sued the solicitor for negligence. It was held by the House of Lords that the solicitor owed a duty of care to the beneficiary and was liable for the economic loss (i.e. the gift in the will). The claimant was a named beneficiary and it was foreseeable she would suffer loss. Imposing liability would not lead to unlimited liability as it only applied to beneficiaries. |

| Case: | |
|---|---|
| **White v Jones** **[1995]** | A 78-year-old testator quarrelled with the claimants, his daughters, and told the defendant solicitors to make a will leaving the daughters out. The testator then made friends with them and told the defendants to make a new will including his daughters. The solicitors delayed and missed meetings with the testator, who then died. The claimants sued for negligence. It was held by a 3/2 majority that the defendants were liable. Otherwise the claimants would have no remedy. |

- The decision does not fit in with the principles under *Hedley Byrne v Heller* [1963] as it is difficult to show that the claimant beneficiaries put reliance on the solicitors or that the solicitors assumed responsibility towards the claimants. It can be explained on the basis that the courts are providing a remedy for the beneficiaries.

## Checkpoint – negligent mis-statements

| Task | Done |
|---|---|
| I can distinguish between the effect of statements made in business and social situations | |
| I understand the two requirements of reasonable reliance | |
| I can explain the two requirements which have to be met for a third party to rely on a statement | |
| I can explain the effect of exclusion clauses in the case of mis-statements | |

# 5.4 Psychiatric injury

## 5.4.1 Distinction between psychiatric injury and mere distress

- The courts have used the term 'nervous shock' which is not a medical term. In modern times it is called 'psychiatric injury'. In order to make a claim in negligence the claimant must prove that they have suffered a recognised psychiatric illness.

- Examples of this include:

  - Post-traumatic stress disorder

  - Pathological grief disorder

  - Clinical depression.

- The law does not allow claims for mere distress or normal grief and everyone is expected to accept these as part of life.

- The claimant must also show that a person of 'normal fortitude' (or ordinary phlegm) would have suffered psychiatric injury in the circumstances. This means someone with normal courage faced with a traumatic event.

## 5.4.2 Brief development of the law

- The original rule was that you could not claim for psychiatric injury in negligence. There was no liability for psychiatric injury unless there was also physical injury (*Victorian Rly Commrs v Coultas* [1888]). The courts were worried both about fraudulent claims and that if they allowed claims, the floodgates would open.

- The courts next allowed a claim by someone who suffered psychiatric harm but who was not injured.

| Case: | |
|---|---|
| ***Dulieu v White* [1901]** | The claimant was working behind the bar in a pub when the defendant negligently drove his horse and van into the pub. The claimant, who was pregnant, suffered psychiatric harm and gave birth prematurely. It was held that if the psychiatric harm arises from fear of personal injury to oneself then a claim could be made. The defendant was liable. |

- The next step was to allow a claim when there was no danger to the claimant. In *Hambrook v Stokes* [1925](CA) a mother had just left her children round a bend in the road when a runaway lorry went round the bend. The mother feared for her children and suffered nervous shock.

- In *McLoughlin v O'Brian* [1983] (HL) a woman was called to a hospital two hours after her family had been involved in a serious road accident and saw them covered in oil and blood. She suffered psychiatric harm and was awarded damages.

## 5.4.3 Distinction between primary and secondary victims

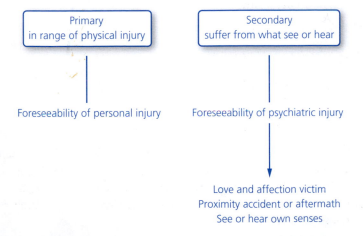

## 5.4.3.1 Primary victims

> **Definition**
>
> Primary victim: someone who is directly involved and within the range of foreseeable personal injury.

| Case: | |
| --- | --- |
| **Page v Smith [1996]** | The defendant negligently drove his car into the claimant's car at low speed. Neither driver suffered any physical injury. The accident caused the claimant's ME to return, which made him very tired and unable to work. The House of Lords said that the claimant was a primary victim and only had to prove that the defendant could foresee 'personal injury' not injury by shock. Personal injury was foreseeable and the defendant was liable. |

- If the victim is within range of physical injury and they suffer psychiatric harm they can claim. They do not have to suffer physical injury.

## 5.4.3.2 Secondary victims

> **Definition**
>
> Secondary victim: someone not directly involved but who suffer from what they see or hear.

- This category of victims is potentially much wider than primary victims, who will be limited to those at risk of physical harm. As a result the law has developed special rules to restrict who may claim. The rules were set out in *Alcock* [1992].

- In *McLoughlin v O'Brian* [1983] in the House of Lords, Lord Wilberforce set out principles which were later developed in *Alcock*. These were the class of persons who could claim; the need for proximity to the accident or aftermath; and the means by which the claimant knew of the event.

| Case: | |
|---|---|
| **Alcock v Chief Constable of South Yorkshire [1992]** | The defendants let too many fans into a football match at the Hillsborough Stadium resulting in the death of 95 people. The claimants included a range of relations and friends. Some were in the football ground, some saw the events live on television or heard it on the radio and some identified bodies at the mortuary. It was held that all the claims failed as they did not meet the criteria set out by the court. |

- The House of Lords set out the three requirements.

### 5.4.3.3 Relationship between the claimant and the victim

- The court did not define the relationships but said that there must be a close relationship of 'love and affection' between the claimant and the victim of the accident.

- There was a presumption of this relationship between spouses, and between parents and children although this presumption could be rebutted. In all other cases the closeness of the relationship had to be proved.

### 5.4.3.4 Proximity of the claimant to the accident or the immediate aftermath

- The claimant must be at the accident or the immediate aftermath. One of the claimants in *Alcock* identified the body of his brother eight hours after the accident but this was not considered sufficient.

### 5.4.3.5 The means by which the shock was caused

- The claimant must see or hear the event or the immediate aftermath with their own unaided senses. If someone was told about the event by a third party, that was not enough.

- Seeing the event on television was not sufficient. Even if this was live the broadcasting code of ethics prohibited showing identifiable individuals. The claims by those who had watched Hillsborough on television therefore failed. The House of Lords left open the possibility of a claim if a disaster was shown live on television (see hot air balloon example of Nolan LJ in the Court of Appeal).

- The claimant must suffer a **sudden shock**. If someone develops a psychiatric injury over a period of time after witnessing an event, that would not satisfy the requirement. But note the effect of the next case on this requirement.

| Case: | |
|---|---|
| **Walters v North Glamorgan NHS Trust [2002]** | The claimant's baby suffered an epileptic fit due to negligent hospital treatment. The baby was transferred to another hospital and the mother followed. The baby was put on life support but this was then switched off and the baby died. These events happened over 36 hours and the claimant suffered psychiatric injury. It was held that it could be treated as one event and the mother had witnessed everything. She was entitled to damages. |

## Rescuers

- If a rescuer suffers only psychiatric injury can they successfully claim?

| Case: | |
|---|---|
| **White v Chief Constable of South Yorkshire [1998]** | The claimants were police officers who all had some part in helping victims at Hillsborough and suffered psychiatric injury. The House of Lords held that rescuers did not have a special position and had to follow the normal rules for primary and secondary victims. They were not in physical danger and not therefore primary victims. Neither could they establish they had a close relationship with the injured so failed as secondary victims. |

- A rescuer is in the same position as any other victim and has to establish that they are either a primary or secondary victim.

## Damage to property

- Can someone claim for psychiatric injury as a result of damage to their **property**?

| Case: | |
|---|---|
| **Attia v British Gas [1987]** | The claimant arranged for British Gas to instal central heating in her house. She went out and when she returned found the house on fire. The fire had been caused by the negligence of British Gas. It was held that it was foreseeable a reasonable house owner would suffer psychiatric injury on seeing their house on fire. |

### Workpoint

L is driving along the main road in his car when M suddenly drives out of a side road and collides with L. L suffers a broken arm and post-traumatic stress disorder.

N, a student, is riding his bicycle along the main road when he is hit by a bus driven by O who is talking on his mobile phone. N is knocked off his bicycle and badly injured. P, N's sister, is on the top deck of the bus and on seeing the accident she screams and suffers shock.

S, N's mother, is told about the accident. S goes to the hospital on the way home from work and when she sees N wrapped in bandages she suffers psychiatric harm.

Advise L, N, P and S of any claims they may make in negligence.

### Research Point

Look up the following article: Teff, H. (2009), Personal Injury: Righting Mental Harms, 159 *NLJ* 1243. It evaluates the current position and makes proposals for reform.

Explain why no reforms to the law on psychiatric harm have been made up to the present time and consider whether the proposals in this article will lead to change.

## Checkpoint – psychiatric injury

| Task | Done |
|------|------|
| I can distinguish between primary and secondary victims | |
| I can list the three requirements from *Alcock* (1992) secondary victims must establish | |
| I can explain the meaning of sudden shock | |
| I understand the legal position of a rescuer who suffers psychiatric injury | |

## Potential exam question

Alex owned an old steam engine and railway carriages. He was driving his empty train into the local station but was travelling too fast. The train came off the rails and tipped over, damaging the railway line. The station and the railway line are owned by Quick Rail plc.

Pieces of broken glass from the accident hit Becki, who was standing on the platform, cutting her face.

Carl lived in a house overlooking the station. On hearing the crash he rushed out to see what had happened and seeing Becki covered in blood, he suffered shock.

A television company was filming the approach of the train and the accident was shown on the television. Becki's mother, Dora, was watching the television and knowing that Becki had gone to the station, Dora suffered post-traumatic stress disorder.

Eric owned a kiosk at the station with trays of sandwiches and cakes on display. Splinters of glass from the accident showered the sandwiches and cakes and Eric had to throw them away. In addition the station had to close for a week while the damaged railway line was repaired and as a result Eric lost a week's profits.

Advise (i) Alex, (ii) Becki, (iii) Carl, (iv) Dora and (v) Eric of the claims they may have in negligence, if any, arising from the above incident.

# Chapter 6

# Liability for defective products

## 6.1 Introduction

- A consumer injured by a defective product has a number of possible ways to claim compensation:

  - Contract

  - Negligence

  - Consumer Protection Act (CPA) 1987.

- It is important to understand the relationship between these three claims and to consider the advantages and disadvantages of each.

- The CPA 1987 was passed to implement the EC Directive 85/374 on product liability. There are some differences in wording between the CPA and the Directive but under the CPA 1987 s1(1) the Act must be interpreted to comply with the Directive. The main purpose of the CPA 1987 was to make it easier for consumers to sue manufacturers without having to prove fault.

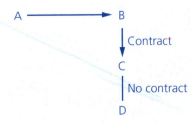

- C buys a coffee maker from B's shop. The coffee maker has been manufactured by A. While D, C's partner, is using it, it bursts into flames due to a manufacturing defect and burns D and sets fire to the kitchen table.

## 6.2 Contract

- If the person injured bought the product they will have a **contract** with the seller and can sue for breach of contract. Liability in contract is strict and the buyer does not have to prove the seller was at fault in any way. The buyer can claim for any damage suffered and for damage to the product itself within the rules of remoteness. They may be able to rely on the terms implied by the Sale of Goods Act 1979.

- If the person injured did not buy the product they cannot sue in contract because of the principle of privity of contract. However, they may be able to sue in contract if they meet the requirements of the Contract (Rights of Third Parties) Act 1999 (C(RTP)A), s1(1)(a), if the contract expressly provides he may, or s1(1)(b) a term purports to give a benefit to the third party.

# 6.3 Negligence

## 6.3.1 Duty, breach and damage

- The claimant (consumer) must prove the three elements of negligence: duty, breach and damage caused.

- In *Donoghue v Stevenson* [1932] the claimant's friend bought her a bottle of ginger beer so only the friend had a contract with the café. The claimant became ill from drinking the ginger beer and sued the manufacturer in negligence. It was held that the manufacturer owed a duty of care to the consumer. This duty is subject to the qualification that there is no possibility of intermediate examination. The ginger beer was in an opaque bottle with a sealed cap and it was impossible for the cafe to check the contents.

- A claim in **negligence** may only be made if the product causes damage. No claim can be made in respect of damage to the product itself.

### 6.3.1.1 Consumer

- The **consumer** covers not only the person using the product but anyone who may forseeably be affected by it.

### 6.3.1.2 Intermediate examination

- If there is an opportunity for **intermediate examination** the manufacturer may not be liable if someone else would be expected to check the product and fails to do so. The mere opportunity to check is not enough, there must be a reasonable probability of inspection.

- Liability may fall on the manufacturer of component parts, repairers, suppliers or even the consumer, for example:

1. a car showroom selling a car would be expected to check that the brakes were working properly (*Andrews v Hopkinson* [1957]).

2. a purchaser of underclothes is not expected to wash them before wearing them (*Grant v Australian Knitting Mills* [1936]).

- The manufacturer may avoid liability by giving a **warning** about use of the product.

| Case: | |
|---|---|
| **Kubach v Hollands [1937]** | A manufacturer sold chemicals to a retailer and gave a warning to test them before use. The retailer sold to a school but did not pass on the warning. A pupil was injured when the chemical exploded. It was held that the manufacturers were not liable but the retailer was negligent. |

**Workpoint**

Alan bought a mobile phone from Beth's phone shop. Beth bought the phone from Chris, a wholesaler. Chris bought the phones in bulk from Don, the manufacturer, but then repackaged them in individual boxes.

A week after buying the phone, due to a manufacturing defect, the phone caught fire and damaged Alan's coffee table.

Explain what claims Alan may make in contract and negligence.

## 6.3.1.3 Causation

- The claimant must prove that the defective product caused the harm. There are particular difficulties proving causation with drugs and complex manufactured goods. This was seen in the thalidomide case in the 1960s. Thalidomide was a drug given to pregnant women and many of them gave birth to deformed babies. The parents sued the manufacturers for negligence but were unable to prove that the drug caused the defects and the matter was settled out of court.

- If the defect in the product is caused after it left the manufacturer, the manufacturer is not negligent. In *Evans v Triplex Glass* [1936] the claimant was injured when his car windscreen shattered. He sued the manufacturer but it was held that the defect could have occurred after the windscreen left the manufacturers e.g. during fitting. The manufacturer was not liable.

## Checkpoint – contract and negligence

| Task | Done |
|---|---|
| I can identify two different legal reasons someone may have a right to sue in contract | |

## Checkpoint – continued

| | |
|---|---|
| I can explain the effect on a claim in negligence of the probability of an intermediate examination | |
| I understand the difficulties of proving causation in negligence | |

# 6.4 Consumer Protection Act 1987

- The CPA 1987 was passed to implement the European Community Directive on Liability for Defective Products 1985.

- Under s2(1) CPA where any damage is caused wholly or partly by a defect in a product, every person to whom subsection (2) applies shall be liable for the damage.

- This imposes strict liability.

- It covers personal injury and damage to property.

**To claim under the CPA you must prove**

1 the product is defective

2 the claimant suffered damage

3 the damage was caused by the defect

## 6.4.1 Product

- Under s1(2) CPA this includes:

  - Goods

  - Electricity

  - Component parts or raw materials incorporated in a finished product

  - Growing crops and things comprised in land by virtue of being attached to it

  - Ship, aircraft or vehicle

  - Primary agricultural products e.g. raw meat, wheat etc.

  - Human blood.

## 6.4.2 Defect

### 6.4.2.1 Section 3

- There is a defect if the safety of the product is not what 'persons generally' are entitled to expect. This has been interpreted to mean the public generally and is an *objective standard* rather than what the *individual consumer* would expect.

- Section 3(2) CPA provides that in deciding if there is a defect courts must take all the circumstances into account including:

  - How the product is marketed, including the packaging, any marks e.g. British Standards Institute (BSI), any instructions on use or warnings.

  - What might 'reasonably be expected' to be done with the product.

  - When the product was supplied by the producer to another. This time is important in deciding if the product is defective, not when it was supplied by the retailer.

  - Manufacturers improve products and this does not make earlier versions defective.

- For example, a manufacturer produces the Mark 2 electric kettle which switches off automatically when it boils. The Mark 1 version did not do that but this fact does not make it a defective product.

| Case: | |
|---|---|
| **Abouzaid v Mothercare Ltd [2000]** | The claimant, aged 12, was fastening a sleeping bag to the back of a pushchair. He stretched the elastic strap of the sleeping bag but it sprung back and the metal buckle hit him in the eye. The Court of Appeal said whether the product was defective was judged by the 'expectations of the public at large'. The product was defective because of the risk of an eye injury. |

- A less strict view of what 'persons generally' were entitled to expect was taken in the next case.

| Case: | |
|---|---|
| **Pollard v Tesco Stores Ltd and Others [2006]** | When the claimant was 13 months old he opened the cap of a bottle of dishwasher powder, ate some and became ill. The powder had been bought from the first defendant and the bottle had been manufactured by the second defendant. The court said that persons generally were entitled to expect it would be more difficult to open than a normal screw cap. Even though it did not meet the BSI level it was more difficult to open than a normal screw cap. There was no legal requirement to reach the BSI level. It was not a defective product and the defendants were not liable. |

### 6.4.3 Damage

- The Act covers:

  - Death

  - Personal injury

  - Property damage if over £275

But not:

  - damage to the product itself

  - economic loss

  - property not ordinarily intended for private use, occupation or consumption (i.e. property for business use).

### 6.4.3.1 Who can sue?

- Anyone who suffers damage and is not limited to the user of the product.

### 6.4.3.2 Who is liable?

- Under s2(1) the 'producer' is liable. This includes those set out in s2(2):

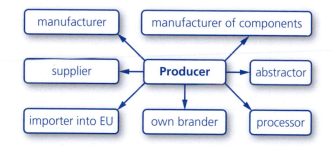

1) Manufacturer;

2) Manufacturer of a component part. If the part is defective both the manufacturer of the product and of the part are liable;

3) Anyone who has 'won or abstracted' the product, e.g. coal;

4) Anyone who processes goods e.g. frozen peas;

5) Own brander. This covers anyone who has 'held himself out' as the producer, e.g. by putting his own name on the product;

6) Importer into the EU. This makes the first person who imports the product into the EU in the course of a business liable;

7) Supplier. If the claimant asks the supplier to identify the producer and they fail to do this within a reasonable time, the supplier is liable.

- The aim of the above provisions is to make it easier for the claimant to find the producer. It is important for anyone in the supply chain to keep a record of who they obtain goods or parts from. e.g. a shop selling to a consumer will be liable if they cannot identify who supplied a defective product to them.

## 6.4.3.3 Defences

- Section 4 CPA sets out the defences.

| s4(1)(a) | Defect due to product complying with a legal requirement. |
|---|---|
| s4(1)(b) | Defendant did not supply the product e.g. goods were stolen. |
| s4(1)(c) | Defendant did not act in the course of a business. |
| s4(1)(d) | Product not defective when supplied e.g. becomes defective through use. |
| s4(1)(e) | Development risks defence – state of knowledge was not enough for a producer to be expected to discover the defect. Art 7 of the Directive provides the defendant must prove that the state of scientific and technical knowledge at the time the producer put the product into circulation was not enough to enable the defect to be discovered. This means that if the knowledge is available to the defendant the defendant is liable. The courts have favoured Art 7 which has a wider meaning than s4(1)(e). In *A v National Blood Authority* [2001] the defendants argued that when the blood was given there was no test to detect hepatitis C and therefore under s4(1)(e) they were not liable. It was held that the defendants knew there was a defect with the blood but continued to supply it and were therefore liable. |
| s4(1)(f) | Defect is in finished product of which component is a part and component is not defective. |

## 6.4.3.4 Exclusion clauses

- A defendant **cannot** exclude liability (s7).

## 6.4.3.5 Limitation

- Any claim for personal injury or damage to property must be brought within three years from when the right of action arose (Limitation Act 1980 s11A).

- A special 'long stop' provision was added by the CPA that any claim under the CPA cannot be brought after 10 years from when the product was supplied. This 10-year period cannot be extended. The idea is to have a time period after which the producer is not liable.

### 6.4.3.6 Summary of liability

|  | Type of liability | Who can sue? | Who is liable? | Type of damage |
|---|---|---|---|---|
| **contract** | strict | buyer; anyone under C(RTP)A 1999 | seller | product itself; injury; other property; economic loss; loss of enjoyment |
| **negligence** | fault | anyone who suffers harm: injury and property | manufacturer | injury; other property |
| **CPA** | strict | anyone who suffers harm: injury and property | producer | injury; other property over £275 |

## Checkpoint – Consumer Protection Act

| Task | Done |
|---|---|
| I can list who can claim under the CPA | |
| I can define what 'product' covers | |
| I can explain the test of 'persons generally' for defective products | |
| I understand what was held in *Pollard v Tesco Ltd* (2006) and why | |
| I understand how the courts have interpreted the development risks defence | |

## Research Point

Please read the section 'Whether a product is defective' in the following article: Lawson, R (2006) The Consumer Protection Act 1987 – two recent cases, 170 *JPN* 544.

It explains the *Pollard* case about the bottle of dishwasher powder with the screw cap.

Explain (i) the argument in the county court that the bottle was a defective product, and (ii) the argument in the Court of Appeal that it was not a defective product under the CPA.

## Workpoint

Please look at the scenario depicted in the figure in 6.1.

Identify the possible claims which could be made and what those claims would cover for (i) C, and (ii) D.

## Potential exam question

Adam lives with his partner Bess and their five-year-old son Cliff. Adam goes to Sam's Supermarket and buys a large tin of beans, a toaster and a water pistol. The beans were the supermarket's own brand. The toaster was manufactured by Don using new electronic controls.

When Adam and Bess are eating the beans they both cut their mouths on splinters of glass which were in the beans. The following day Bess was using the toaster when it burst into flames. Bess was burned and the kitchen worktop was badly damaged. It was later discovered that the electronic controls had malfunctioned.

Cliff started playing with the water pistol but it began leaking and Bess discovered that it had a hole in it.

Explain what action may be taken, if any, in respect of (i) the beans, (ii) the toaster and (iii) the water pistol.

# Chapter 7

# Nuisance

## 7.1 Introduction

PRIVATE

PUBLIC STATUTORY

- There are three types of nuisance: private nuisance, public nuisance and statutory nuisance. There is some overlap between all three.

- A **private nuisance** protects an individual's interest in land from physical damage and from interference with their enjoyment of land. A private nuisance is a tort.

- A **public nuisance** protects the public or a class of the public from certain actions. There is no need to have an interest in land. A public nuisance is a crime. If someone suffers as a result they may be able to claim in tort.

- A **statutory nuisance** is defined in the **Environmental Protection Act 1990** and covers a wide range of matters such as smoke, dust, fumes and noise. Such nuisances are controlled by the local authority issuing an order to stop the nuisance.

- The tort of nuisance overlaps with negligence, trespass to land and *Rylands v Fletcher*.

## 7.2 Who can sue and be sued?

### 7.2.1 Who can sue?

- The aim of private nuisance is to protect a person's interest in land. In order to sue, someone has to have an interest in land, for example, the owner or tenant of land. This means that a lodger, a guest and the spouse or children of the landowner have no right to sue in nuisance because they do not have an interest in land.

| Case: | |
| --- | --- |
| ***Malone v Laskey* [1907]** | Mrs Malone was injured when a toilet cistern fell on her as a result of vibrations from next door. Her claim in nuisance failed as she had no interest in the property as she was merely a licensee. |

- The need to have a proprietary interest (i.e ownership) in land was confirmed by the House of Lords in the following case.

| Case: | |
| --- | --- |
| ***Hunter v Canary Wharf* [1997]** | Some of the claimants were owners but others included spouses, children and lodgers. It was held that only those with a proprietary interest in the land or someone with a right to exclusive possession could sue in nuisance. The court also confirmed that no claim could be made in nuisance for personal injury and such a claim would have to be in negligence. |

## 7.2.2 Who can be sued?

### 7.2.2.1 The creator

- Any person who does a positive act, rather than an omission, which creates a nuisance can be held liable.

### 7.2.2.2 The occupier

- An occupier is liable for a nuisance that they create and may also be liable for the actions of those they control, previous occupiers and even trespassers. Therefore an occupier will be liable for the acts of employees. An occupier will only be liable for the acts of trespassers if they 'adopt or continue' the nuisance.

| Case: | |
|---|---|
| *Sedleigh-Denfield v O'Callaghan* **[1940]** | The defendants owned a ditch and the local authority trespassed and laid a pipe in the ditch but forgot to put a grid on the end of the pipe. The defendants knew about the pipe and used it to drain water from their land. Some years later the pipe became blocked and flooded the claimant's land. It was held that by using the pipe the defendants had continued and adopted the nuisance and were liable to the claimant in nuisance. |

### 7.2.2.3 The landowner

- The general rule is that if the landowner parts with possession of the land the landowner is not liable for a nuisance. The landowner can be liable if the nuisance started before the land was let or the landowner authorised the nuisance.

| Case: | |
|---|---|
| *Tetley v Chitty and Others* **[1986]** | The local authority let land in a residential area to the defendant to be used for a go-karting club. The neighbours brought an action in nuisance because of the noise. The court said that letting the land for go-karting meant that noise was an inevitable result and was effectively authorising the nuisance. The council was liable. |

# 7.3 Private nuisance

> **Definition**
>
> Private nuisance: an unlawful act which indirectly
>
> - causes physical damage to land, or
> - interferes with enjoyment of land, or
> - interferes with interests in land, and
>
> which is unreasonable taking into account all the circumstances.

- The harm caused by the defendant's act must be indirect rather than a direct result of the act, for example, smoke caused by a fire which interferes with the enjoyment of land.

- The tort of nuisance tries to balance the rights of neighbouring landowners to use their land without affecting one another too much.

- **Point to note:** private nuisance can apply to a 'one off' event and does not have to be a continuing act.

## 7.3.1 Physical damage

- The claimant must suffer 'material injury' to their property.

Note that if the property is abnormally sensitive a claim would fail (see 7.3.3.2 below).

| Case: |  |
|-------|--|
| *St Helens Smelting Co v Tipping* **(1865)** | Fumes from the defendant's copper smelting works caused damage to trees growing in the claimant's garden. The House of Lords held that the claimant had proved physical damage to land and the defendant was liable in nuisance. The court said that the fact it was an industrial area was irrelevant if there was physical damage to land. |

## 7.3.2 Interference with the use and enjoyment of land

- The law has to balance the right of a landowner to use their land as they wish with the right of a neighbouring landowner to use their land. An activity only becomes a nuisance if it is unreasonable in all the circumstances.

- The law protects a wide range of interests of landowners but new interests may be recognised. Established interests include:

  - noise

  - smoke

  - smells

  - a sex shop in a residential street.

### 7.3.2.1 Does private nuisance protect someone from personal injury?

- It protects interests in land and does not extend to **personal injury** (*Hunter v Canary Wharf* (1997)).

### 7.3.2.2 Does the law of nuisance protect the right to receive television signals?

- In *Hunter v Canary Wharf* (1997) the House of Lords said that no claim could be made in nuisance for interference with television reception caused by a tall building. However the question was left open whether something else interfering with television reception would be a nuisance.

## 7.3.3 The test of unreasonableness

- In deciding if a person's use of land is unreasonable the courts take a number of factors into account. These are only considered if they are relevant to the individual case and the decision is made on balance whether the activity is unreasonable.

### 7.3.3.1 Locality

- Where the act occurs is relevant in deciding whether it is a nuisance. A factory in an industrial area will not be a nuisance to neighbours but would be in a residential area.

| Case: | |
|---|---|
| ***Sturges v Bridgman* (1879)** | The claimant doctor worked in a residential area which had a number of other doctors. He built a consulting room but complained about the noise from the defendant's biscuit factory next door. It was held that the defendant's actions were a nuisance because it was an area of medical specialists. Thesiger LJ said '...what would be a nuisance in Belgrave Square would not necessarily be so in Bermondsey'. |

- The character of an area can change and this will affect the decision whether an activity was a nuisance or not.

| Case: | |
|---|---|
| ***Gillingham Borough Council v Medway Dock Co* [1992]** | The council granted planning permission to change a naval docks into a commercial port, which operated 24 hours a day. Some years later the council wished to restrict traffic because the noise was a public nuisance. Held that the character of the area had to be judged after the planning permission was given and the noise was not a nuisance. |

## 7.3.3.2 Sensitivity

- The test is whether the defendant's use of property is reasonable. If the claimant or the claimant's property is abnormally sensitive then the defendant's action will not be a nuisance.

| Case: | |
|---|---|
| **Robinson v Kilvert [1889]** | The defendant manufactured boxes in a cellar and the heat from the process made the floor above reach 80°F (about 27°C). The claimant stored sensitive brown paper on the floor above and this was damaged by the heat. The heat would not have affected ordinary paper. The court held that the defendant was not liable for nuisance. |

- If the claimant can show that the defendant's actions would have damaged ordinary property then a claim can be made for sensitive property.

| Case: | |
|---|---|
| **McKinnon Industries v Walker [1951]** | Sulphur dioxide gas from McK's factory damaged delicate orchids grown by W. It was held that the gas would have damaged ordinary flowers and therefore it was a nuisance. |

- More recently the Court of Appeal has questioned the use of this factor of sensitivity and instead relied on the test of foreseeability.

| Case: | |
|---|---|
| **Network Rail Ltd v Morris (t/a Soundstar Studio) [2004]** | NR installed new electronic signalling equipment on its rail track which caused electromagnetic interference with M's recording studio 80 metres away and he lost business. He sued for nuisance. The Court of Appeal accepted that use of electronic equipment is part of modern life. But it was difficult to apply the principle of sensitivity where both parties had competing use of such equipment. The key to the relationship was the test of reasonableness and it was better to use the test of foreseeability to determine this rather than sensitivity. It was not foreseeable that interference from the signalling equipment would affect M's activities 80 metres away. No one else had complained. C's claim failed. |

### 7.3.3.3 Malice

- If a property owner does an act with malice, intending to cause a nuisance that may make the act unreasonable and a nuisance. But malice will not necessarily make the act a nuisance (see *Bradford Corporation v Pickles* [1895](HL)).

| Case: | |
|---|---|
| ***Christie v Davey*** **[1893]** | The claimants and defendant lived in adjoining semi-detached houses in Brixton. Mrs Christie gave music lessons and most of the family played musical instruments. The defendant complained about the noise but was ignored. He then took to banging on the wall with a tray and blowing a whistle whenever he heard music. It was held that as the defendant's acts were done deliberately they amounted to a nuisance and an injunction was granted. |

### 7.3.3.4 Duration

- How long the interference goes on is relevant in deciding if it is a nuisance. The longer it goes on, the more likely it will be a nuisance. Nuisance is usually seen as continuing but this is not necessary and something which carries on for a short period can still be a nuisance.

- For example, a party lasting until 3.00am would probably not be a nuisance but if the property owner held one five nights a week that may well be!

### 7.3.3.5 Public benefit

- Something which is a benefit to the public may be seen as reasonable and not a nuisance. It is difficult to establish a public benefit, as shown in the Irish case of *Bellew v Irish Cement Co* [1948] in which a cement factory was closed because it was a nuisance, even though it provided most of the country's cement.

| Case: | |
|---|---|
| ***Adams v Ursell*** **[1913]** | The defendant opened a fish and chip shop in a residential street and the claimants, who lived next door complained about the fog and steam which filled their house. It was held that even though there was some benefit to the public it was a private nuisance and an injunction was granted. |

## Interference with interests in land

- A landowner has various rights such as a right of support of their land from neighbouring land and a right to light. They may also have rights over neighbouring land such as a right of way. Interference with such rights will be a private nuisance.

## Natural condition of the land

- Originally a landowner was not liable for a nuisance caused by the natural condition of the land or an act of nature, for example, lightning causing a fire which spreads to neighbouring land. The law has changed in recent years.

| Case: | |
|---|---|
| **Leakey v National Trust [1980]** | The claimant owned two houses at the bottom of the defendant's hill. Natural subsidence caused rocks to fall down the hill towards the houses. The defendant knew about this but took no action to stop it. It was held that if the defendant knew about the risk he had to do what was reasonable to prevent damage. A subjective standard was applied to the defendant taking into account their finances, abilities, etc. The defendant was liable in nuisance. |

- In the next case the courts considered the issue of support of land and said that a duty could exist in law to prevent foreseeable damage.

| Case: | |
|---|---|
| **Holbeck Hall Hotel v Scarborough Borough Council [2000]** | The claimant owned a hotel on the cliffs which were owned by the council. The cliffs were being eroded by the sea. In 1993 part of the hotel fell into the sea. The court said that if a landowner knows about the nuisance they have a duty to prevent foreseeable damage. Here the extent of the damage was not foreseeable without an expensive geological survey and as there was no duty to have a survey, the defendant was not liable. |

### Workpoint

Ali owns a semi-detached house in a residential street and Bill owns the house next door. Ali frequently lights bonfires in his garden to burn newspapers and old rubber hosepipes. Smoldering fragments of the

*Continued overleaf*

newspapers land on the roof of Bill's garden shed causing burn marks. Thick black smoke from the fires drifts into Bill's house.

Clive lives next to a fire station. He is often woken up by fire engines driving in and out of the fire station during the night, with their sirens sounding.

Donna lives in a quiet village. She complained to Eric, her next door neighbour, about his cockerel crowing at 6.00am every day and waking her. Since she complained Eric has done nothing about the cockerel and has started banging on a tin tray with a hammer until midnight, several nights a week.

1) Identify the nature of the private nuisance(s) in each case and identify any relevant factor from the test of unreasonableness.

2) Briefly explain whether the activity amounts to a nuisance in each case.

## Checkpoint – requirements for private nuisance

| Task | Done |
|---|---|
| I can define private nuisance | |
| I can distinguish nuisance by physical damage to land and nuisance by interference with enjoyment | |
| I can explain the test of unreasonableness and the five factors | |
| I can distinguish *Robinson v Kilvert* (1889) and *McKinnon Industries v Walker* (1951) | |
| I can explain a landowner's liability in nuisance for the natural condition of land | |

# 7.4 Defences

• The defences of prescription and statutory authority have been used successfully. Other successful defences are consent and contributory negligence (see Chapter 14).

• Other defences have been argued but have not been successful, public benefit of the defendant's act and that the claimant came to the nuisance.

| Prescription | If the defendant carries on a private nuisance for 20 years they will acquire the legal right to commit that nuisance by 'prescription' i.e. right by long use. It is not enough to show that the defendant did the act for 20 years it must be a nuisance for that period. *Sturges v Bridgman* [1879] Although the defendant had been operating his factory for over 20 years the nuisance did not start until the claimant doctor built his surgery. The defendant could not therefore claim a prescriptive right to make noise. |
|---|---|
| Statutory Authority | A statute may authorise a particular activity and provide that doing the activity is not a nuisance. If a statute does not say anything about nuisance it will have to be interpreted. *Allen v Gulf Oil* [1981](HL) A statute gave the defendant the power to build a refinery but it did not give power to operate it. When the refinery was built residents complained that the smell and noise was a nuisance. It was held that Parliament must have intended that the refinery could be operated and anything which was an inevitable result of that was not a nuisance. The claimant's case failed. |
| Public Benefit | It is difficult to establish that a nuisance should be allowed because it is a benefit to the public. This was seen in *Adams v Ursell* [1913]. In *Dennis v Ministry of Defence* [2003] the claimant lived near an RAF base and complained about the noise. The court said that the public benefit of training pilots took precedence over the claimant's private rights not to commit a nuisance. But under Article 8 (right to private life) the claimant was entitled to damages. (See section 7.5). |
| Coming to the Nuisance | Defendants have argued that they are not liable in nuisance because the claimant chose to come and live near the nuisance and has effectively consented to it. This is not a defence. In *Miller v Jackson* [1977] (CA) the defendant cricket club had played cricket for over 70 years when some houses were built next to it. The claimant bought one of the houses and complained that balls landing in his garden were a nuisance. The court had to balance the public interest in playing cricket and the private interest of the claimant. The court decided by a 2/1 majority that it was no defence that the claimant had come to the nuisance. The defendant was liable in nuisance and had to pay damages but an injunction was refused. |

Fred owns a two bedroom terraced house. Gail comes to stay as a lodger and pays £100 a week rent. Harry owns the house next door and has started playing his electric guitar early every morning. This wakes Gail up.

Ivy owned a field on the edge of a village. Jon entered a 12-month tenancy agreement with Ivy for the field to be used to graze sheep. Keith's house is next to the field. Recently Keith has been disturbed by the noise of Jon racing around the field on his motorbike.

Len bought a house overlooking the ground of his local football team Mellow FC. The club have played football at the ground for 50 years. A few months after buying the house Len has become annoyed because footballs keep landing in his garden and on a couple of occasions have broken his windows.

1) Advise Gail and Keith about who they may sue, if anyone, in private nuisance.

2) Advise Mellow FC whether they have any defence to a claim of nuisance by Len.

# 7.5 Nuisance and human rights

• Apart from a claim in private nuisance a claim may be made under Article 8(1) for interference with private and family life. This right may be restricted by Article 8(2) for the protection of others or in the public interest. In *Dennis v Ministry of Defence* [2003] noise from planes at an RAF base was held to be a nuisance and a breach of Article 8(1). Although damages were awarded in nuisance an injunction was refused because the public interest in flying was greater than the private interests of the claimant.

• There is no need to have an interest in land to claim under the Human Rights Act (HRA) 1998. But the HRA 1998 only applies to public bodies.

## Checkpoint – private nuisance: liability, defences and human rights

| Task | Done |
|---|---|
| I can explain who has the right to sue for private nuisance | |
| I can identify three groups of people who may be made liable for private nuisance | |

**Checkpoint – continued**

| Task | Done |
|---|---|
| I understand the requirements for the defence of prescription to apply | |
| I can explain the case of *Miller v Jackson* (1977) (CA) | |
| I understand the relationship of Article 8 to private nuisance | |

# 7.6 Public nuisance

- A public nuisance is a crime and the person responsible for it can be prosecuted.

**Definition**

> Public nuisance: an act or omission 'which materially affects the reasonable comfort and convenience of life of a class of Her Majesty's subjects'.

- Lord Denning said that it was something so widespread that it would not be reasonable to expect one person to take action to stop it.

- The same act may be both a public nuisance and a private nuisance.

| Case: | |
|---|---|
| ***Attorney General v PYA Quarries Ltd* [1957]** | The defendants operated a quarry and noise, vibrations and dust affected people living nearby. It was held that this amounted to a public nuisance. |

- Public nuisance covers a wide range of activities and examples include blocking a public road, selling food which is unfit for human consumption.

- The activity must affect the public or a class of the public. This is an important difference to private nuisance. How many people constitute a 'class' is a question of fact. In *R v Johnson* [1996] the Court of Appeal said that making obscene phone calls to 13 women was enough to be a public nuisance. However, in *R v Rimmington* [2006] the defendant sent racially abusive letters to over 500 individuals. The House of Lords said that this was not a public nuisance as a section of the public had to be affected by the nuisance.

| Case: | |
|---|---|
| **Halsey v Esso [1961]** | The claimant lived opposite the defendant's oil depot in Fulham and complained about: (i) acid smuts damaging washing on the line; (ii) the smell of oil; (iii) noise from the boilers; (iv) noise from lorries in the depot; (v) acid smuts damaging the claimant's car on the road; and (vi) noise from lorries going into the depot. The court said that noise at night was particularly significant as most people were in bed. (i)–(iv) were private nuisances and (v) and (vi) were public nuisances. |

## 7.6.1 Action in tort for public nuisance

• If an individual can show that they have suffered 'special damage' over and above the public or a class of the public they can sue the defendant in the tort of public nuisance. The particular damage may consist of financial loss, physical damage to property or personal injury. There is no need to have an interest in land to bring a claim in public nuisance.

| Case: | |
|---|---|
| **Tate & Lyle Ltd v GLC [1983]** | The defendant built a ferry terminal which caused the river to silt up. The court held that this interfered with the general right of navigation and was a public nuisance. The claimants had suffered particular damage because they had to dredge the area round their jetty and the defendant was liable for public nuisance. |

• If an individual cannot show that they have suffered special damage they can ask the Attorney General for permission to start civil proceedings, known as a relator action. This may lead to the granting of an injunction to stop the nuisance.

### Workpoint

Neil, a lorry driver, sometimes parks his lorry in the street where he lives. This annoys his neighbour Olive because the lorry sometimes blocks her driveway. Many of the residents have complained that the lorry blocks the street.

Advise Olive and the residents of any action they may take in nuisance.

# 7.7 Distinctions between private and public nuisance

| Private nuisance | Public nuisance |
|---|---|
| a tort only | a crime and a tort |
| need interest in land to sue | no need for an interest in land |
| cannot claim for personal injury | can claim for personal injury |
| defence of prescription | no prescription |
| only need one person affected | must affect public or a class of people |

## Checkpoint – public nuisance

| Task | Done |
|---|---|
| I can define public nuisance | |
| I understand when someone can sue in tort for a public nuisance | |
| I can identify the distinctions between private and public nuisance | |

# 7.8 Statutory nuisance

• There are many statutes which provide that certain actions amount to a statutory nuisance. They give the local authority power to take action to stop the nuisance. The local authority can serve a notice on the person responsible to stop the nuisance (abate). Failure to do so can result in a fine.

• An example would be making noise in a residential area after a certain time.

## Research Point

Look up the following article: Foster, N. (2010), Civil Liability Arising from the Buncefield Explosion, *Enviro LR* 12 1 (57).

Identify which groups of people could bring actions:

(i) for private nuisance;

*Continued overleaf*

**Research Point – continued**

(ii)  public nuisance; and

(iii)  under *Rylands v Fletcher* (see also Chapter 8).

# 7.9 Remedies for nuisance

## 7.9.1 Damages

- A claimant who successfully sues in private nuisance is entitled to damages for the harm to the land. This can include loss of profits and loss of value of the land.

## 7.9.2 Injunctions

- This is a very important remedy in nuisance as damages would not be sufficient if the defendant continued with the nuisance. An injunction is an equitable remedy and is granted at the discretion of the court. In *Kennaway v Thompson* [1980](CA) the court granted an injunction to restrict powerboat racing on a lake which affected the claimant's house overlooking the lake.

## 7.9.3 Abatement

- The person affected by a nuisance has a right to stop (or abate) the nuisance. It could be used for example if the defendant's tree roots or branches encroach on the claimant's land.

**Potential exam question**

Some years ago Adam bought a house on the outskirts of the town of Northville in a quiet street which overlooked the countryside. He lived there with his wife Bev and her elderly mother Celia. Dai, who was interested in old railway steam engines, owned a large field in the countryside behind Adam's house. Northville Council granted Dai planning permission to build a miniature railway line in the field and to operate a miniature steam engine.

The railway consisted of a station and a circular track of approximately one kilometre. While it was being built the noise from the building works disturbed Celia's afternoon nap.

When the railway opened Dai operated it every weekend to give rides to visitors who were mainly children. Adam complained about the noise from the steam engine and from the children. The noise lasted all day from 9.00am until 6.00pm in the evening. Adam complained to Dai about this noise but after this Dai blew the train's whistle at 7.00am each morning.

Clouds of smoke and ash from the steam engine drifted over the neighbouring houses and into Adam's garden and damaged a number of plants including some delicate orchids being grown by Bev. Bev also developed a sore throat from the smoke and needed medical treatment from her family doctor.

During holiday times the railway was so busy that visitors would cause traffic jams in the street which would sometimes last an hour. This annoyed the residents and on one occasion Adam was unable to leave his driveway for an hour and was late arriving to watch his local football team.

Advise (i) Adam, (ii) Bev, (iii) Celia and (iv) the residents of the action they may take, if any, in nuisance in respect of the above incidents.

# Chapter 8

## Rylands v Fletcher

## 8.1 Introduction

- A distinction is made in tort between **fault liability** and **strict liability**:

  - Fault liability – someone is only liable if they are at fault in some way, e.g. acting negligently.

  - Strict liability – even though someone has not done anything wrong (i.e. there is no fault) they are liable. The principle of strict liability applies in some statutes and in the rule in *Rylands v Fletcher*.

| Case: | |
|---|---|
| ***Rylands v Fletcher*** (1865) | The defendant mill owner took on an independent contractor to build a reservoir on the defendant's land. The contractor discovered some disused mine shafts but did not block them up. When the reservoir was filled with water, it went down the mine shafts and flooded the claimant's mine. The defendant did not know about the mine shafts. It was held that the defendant was liable even though he was not to blame. |

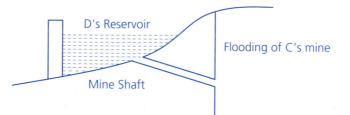

- The rule in *Rylands v Fletcher* was set out by Blackburn J at first instance:

*'… the person who, for his own purposes, brings on his land and collects and keeps there anything likely to do mischief if it escapes, must keep it in at his peril; and if he does not do so, is prima facie answerable for all the damage which is the natural consequence of its escape'.*

- The House of Lords added that the defendant's use of land must be non-natural.

- The principle of strict liability has some defences available.

- *Rylands v Fletcher* must be considered alongside nuisance. They both deal with activities on land which affect other land. To sue under these torts a person needs an interest in land.

# 8.2 Requirements for liability

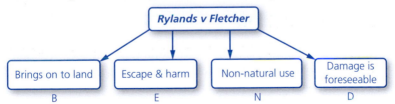

## 8.2.1 Brings onto land something likely to do mischief

- The defendant must bring something on to his land. There is no liability for things which are naturally on the land e.g. weeds growing naturally which are blown from the defendant's land on to neighbouring land.

- It must be something which is likely to do mischief. This covers not only inherently dangerous things e.g. chemicals, gas, electricity, fire, explosives, a lion, etc. but also normally safe things which can cause damage if they escape e.g. water, strips of metal foil. In *Transco plc v Stockport MBC* [2003] Lord Bingham said that it had to be shown that the defendant ought to have recognised that there was 'an exceptionally high risk of danger or mischief if there should be an escape'.

## 8.2.2 It escapes and causes harm

- There must be an escape from the defendant's land.

| Case: | |
|---|---|
| *Read v Lyons* [1947] | The claimant munitions inspector was visiting the defendant's munitions factory when a shell exploded and she was injured. The defendants had not acted negligently. It was held that there was no escape and the defendant was not liable under *Rylands v Fletcher.* |

- The thing that escapes need not be the thing brought on to land e.g. explosives which cause rocks to be blown on to the claimant's land will fall under the rule.

- The escape must cause damage to property as personal injury is not covered. A claim for personal injury could be made in negligence.

## 8.2.3 Non-natural use of land

- The claimant must establish that the defendant's use of land is non-natural.

- 'Non-natural' use means something which is not an ordinary use of land. What is an 'ordinary' use will depend on all the circumstances.

- What is ordinary use will also change over time e.g. using electricity for domestic purposes is now an ordinary use but would not have been 100 years ago.

- In *Rickards v Lothian* [1913] Lord Moulton said that the use of land must bring increased danger to others and is not merely ordinary use or use for 'the general benefit of the community'.

- However, in *Cambridge Water Co Ltd v Eastern Counties Leather* [1994] Lord Goff said that storing chemicals in industrial premises was a 'non-natural' use. He added that if something was a benefit to the community it did not make it a natural use.

- In *Transco plc v Stockport Metropolitan Borough Council* [2003] Lord Hoffmann said that in deciding if something is a non-natural use, ask if the damage was something which the occupier could reasonably be expected to have insured against. The result would be that if insurance should have been taken out it would not be a non-natural use.

## 8.2.4 Damage is foreseeable

- The original rule imposed strict liability. The decision in the next case added the requirement that damage had to be foreseeable.

| Case: | |
|---|---|
| *Cambridge Water Co Ltd v Eastern Counties Leather plc* [1994] | The defendant leather company used a chemical solvent in its tanning process until 1976. Over the years some of this was spilt on the concrete floor. The chemical seeped into the soil and went into the claimant's borehole, which was over one mile away (over one kilometre) from the tannery and contaminated the water. The contamination was only discovered in 1983 when new regulations required testing the water. The claimants had to drill a new borehole at a cost of £1m. The House of Lords said that to claim under *Rylands v Fletcher* foreseeability of damage had to be proved. At the time the solvent was brought onto the land the defendants could not foresee that it would damage the claimant's water supply and the defendants were not liable. |

- The test of **foreseeability** is that at the time the thing was brought onto the land the defendant had to foresee that, if it escaped, it would cause the particular type of damage which was suffered. In the *Cambridge Water* case it was foreseeable that the solvent might cause some damage but not damage to the claimant's water supply over a mile away.

# 8.3 Defences

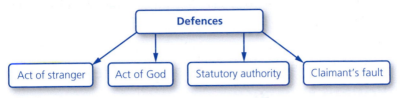

## 8.3.1 Act of a stranger

- If the damage was caused by the act of a third party and the defendant had no control over them, the defendant will not be liable.

| Case: | |
|---|---|
| **Rickards v Lothian [1913]** | The claimant occupied the second floor in a building leased to the defendant. One night a third party turned on a tap on the fourth floor and blocked the overflow of the sink. The water damaged the claimant's goods. It was held that the defendant was not liable for the wrongful act of the third party. |

- If the defendant could have foreseen the act of the third party the defence fails.

## 8.3.2 Act of God

- If the escape is caused by natural forces and could not have been foreseen this is a good defence e.g. lightning, earthquake, exceptional rain storm.

## 8.3.3 Statutory authority

- If a defendant acts under a statute, the statute may provide a defence.

## 8.3.4 Claimant's fault

- If the escape is due to the claimant's own act the defendant is not liable.

- If the escape is partly due to the claimant's act damages may be reduced for contributory negligence.

## Checkpoint – *Rylands v Fletcher*

| Task | Done |
|---|---|
| I can define the tort of *Rylands v Fletcher* | |
| I can identify and explain the requirements for liability under *Rylands v Fletcher* | |
| I can explain four defences available | |
| I understand the decision in *Rickards v Lothian* (1913) | |

# 8.4 Comparison of *Rylands v Fletcher* and Private Nuisance

| *Rylands v Fletcher* | Private Nuisance |
|---|---|
| Need an interest in land | Need an interest in land |
| Can not claim for personal injury | Can not claim for personal injury |
| Need foreseeability of harm | Need foreseeability of harm |
| Need an escape from land | No need for an escape from land |
| Liability for a single event | Single event or continuous act |

## Research Point

Read the judgment of Lord Hoffmann in *Transco plc v Stockport MBC* [2003] (HL).

1) Explain the historical background to the case of *Rylands v Fletcher.*

2) Explain whether or not damages can be claimed for personal injury under *Rylands v Fletcher.*

3) Explain the five points Lord Hoffmann makes as regards the application of *Rylands v Fletcher* today.

Look up the following article: Waite, A.J. (2006), Deconstructing the Rule in *Rylands v Fletcher. J Environmental Law* 18 (3), 423.

1) Explain the difference between the narrow rule in *Rylands v Fletcher* and the wide rule in *Rylands v Fletcher.*

2) Identify the five reasons put forward by the author why the principle of strict liability should be used to control dangerous activities.

## Potential exam question

Anoil are a specialist producer of fuels for both commercial and domestic use. They operate from a large site which is surrounded by a three-metre-high fence. The site is on the edge of a town.

Ben, a factory inspector, arrives at the site and parks his car on the road outside. As he is walking towards the main entrance there is an explosion on the site and the blast knocks Ben to the ground injuring him and damaging his car. The explosion was caused by fumes escaping from a faulty valve.

One building on the site is used for producing aviation fuel some of which is sold to airlines and some to the RAF for use in bombers. The following day there is an explosion in this building. Debris from the blast lands on Colin's house, which is in the road next to the site, damaging his roof.

One night Dick climbs over the fence looking for things to steal. He opens the tap on a large storage tank. Oil flows out and floods a nearby street and it runs into Eli's garden ruining all her plants.

Advise (i) Ben, (ii) Colin and (iii) Eli of any action they may take in respect of the above incidents.

# Chapter 9
## Trespass to land

## 9.1 Requirements for trespass

> **Definition**
>
> Trespass to land: a direct and unlawful interference with another person's possession of land.

- Trespass is actionable *per se* and there is no need to prove damage to the land.

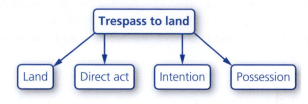

### 9.1.1 Land
- Land includes:
  - the surface of the land
  - things attached to the land e.g. buildings, trees, crops
  - the airspace above the land
  - the ground below the surface.

- Any intrusion into the airspace may be a trespass e.g. a crane swinging over another's land (*Anchor Brewhouse Developments v Berkley House* [1987]). However, the rights to the airspace extend only to a height necessary for ordinary use.

| Case: | |
|---|---|
| ***Bernstein v Skyviews Ltd* [1977]** | The defendants flew over the claimant's land in a small plane taking aerial photographs. The claimant argued that this was trespass to land. It was held that as it was hundreds of metres above the ground it did not interfere with the claimant's use of land and was not a trespass. |

- The rights extend to the subsoil beneath the surface. In *Bocardo SA v Star Energy UK* [2010] the defendant had been given a licence to drill for oil by the Crown. The defendant put pipelines between 800 and 2,800 feet under the claimant's land. The Supreme Court held that this was a trespass but awarded only nominal damages.

## 9.1.2 Direct

- The act must be a **direct** interference with the land e.g. walking across your neighbour's lawn. Other examples would be throwing something on to land or staying on land when permission to be there has ended.

- An indirect act would not be trespass e.g. allowing a tree to overgrow a neighbour's land, but a nuisance.

## 9.1.3 Intention

- The act must be **intentional**. If someone walks on to another's land by mistake that is still an intentional act and is a trespass. A person does not have to have the intention to trespass, just an intention to do the act. If someone's animals stray on to another person's land that may be trespass.

| Case: | |
|---|---|
| *League Against Cruel Sports v Scott* [1985] | The claimant owned some unfenced moorland. The defendant was the master of a hunt and the hounds strayed on to the claimant's land on a number of occasions. The court said that it was trespass if the master intended the hounds to enter or was negligent in allowing them to enter or even if it was impossible to stop the hounds entering, intention could be shown by hunting in that area. This was a trespass to land. |

## 9.1.4 Possession

- The tort of trespass protects the right to **possession** of land and it is not necessary to be the owner to claim. The claimant must have possession of the land. This is not simply physical possession of the land, the claimant must have the right to exclude others. e.g a landlord. A lodger does not have a right of exclusive possession and cannot sue for trespass.

# 9.2 Other points

## 9.2.1 A continuing act

- A trespass may consist of:

  1. a single act e.g. walking across someone's land, or

  2. a continuing act e.g. throwing rubbish on to another's land – the trespass continues until the rubbish is removed.

## 9.2.2 Trespass *ab initio*

- If someone has permission of the occupier to enter land but goes beyond that permission they become a trespasser from that point in time e.g. a customer in a shop who goes behind the shop counter, becomes a trespasser at that point.

- If someone has permission to enter land under a statutory or common law power rather than the permission of the occupier but they do an act which is beyond that power, a rule known as trespass *ab initio* applies. The rule only applies to acts not omissions. The person is regarded as trespassing *from the point of entry* not the point they act beyond the power. The courts have shown that a partial abuse of power is not enough for this rule to apply.

| Case: | |
|---|---|
| *Elias v Pasmore* **[1934]** | The defendant police officers entered the claimant's premises with a lawful warrant to arrest H. They seized some documents relevant to H's trial and some which were not. It was held that it was unlawful to seize the irrelevant documents. But the defendants were not trespassers to land *ab initio* because they had a lawful warrant to enter to arrest H. |

## 9.2.3 Highways

- A public road (or highway) is owned by the local highway authority. The land underneath the road is owned by the adjoining land owners. The public have a right of passage over the highway. This was originally a rather limited right which covered incidental purposes e.g. stopping for a rest. But using the highway for other purposes was trespass.

| Case: | |
|---|---|
| **Hickman v Maisey [1900]** | The claimant owned land with a highway running across it and he allowed a racehorse trainer to train horses on the land. The defendant, a racing journalist, walked up and down the highway for an hour and a half, making notes about the horses. It was held that the defendant's activity had exceeded reasonable use and was trespass to land. |

- In *DPP v Jones* [1999] the House of Lords said that a public highway can be used for 'any reasonable purpose' as long as it did not obstruct the highway or cause a public or private nuisance. A peaceful assembly of 20 people on a road which met these points was not therefore a trespass. This decision extends the law as it allows people to do more than merely pass along the highway but exactly what it now covers remains to be seen.

## Workpoint

Ann lives in a detached house which is next to her neighbour Bob's house. Ann is an engineer and she is conducting research on tunnelling methods. She develops a small boring machine which is 10 centimetres in diameter. She uses it to drill down five metres in her garden and then drill under Bob's house. The trial is successful and no damage is caused.

Ann keeps six sheep in her back garden. The garden backs on to Don's farm. The sheep escape through a hole in the fence into Don's farm and eat some of his crops.

Felix owns a house on the corner of a street and the front garden is unfenced. Eve signs a six-month tenancy for the house. A few weeks after moving in Eve notices that George, who lives down the street, sometimes takes a short cut across the front garden instead of following the public pavement.

Advise Bob, Don, Eve and Felix whether or not they have a right to sue for trespass to land.

## Checkpoint – requirements for a claim for trespass to land

| Task | Done |
|---|---|
| I can identify the four requirements to claim trespass to land | |

## Checkpoint – continued

| Task | Done |
|---|---|
| I can explain what 'land' covers | |
| I can distinguish a direct act to land from an indirect act | |
| I understand the significance of *DPP v Jones* (1999) for rights on the highway | |

# 9.3 Defences

## 9.3.1 Consent

- A person in possession of land may give consent to another to enter the land. This consent is known as a licence. A licence may be given expressly or it may be implied.

- **Express consent** would be inviting a friend to visit you.

- **Implied consent** would be a sales person walking up your garden path.

- A licence may be a bare licence – no payment is made; or a contractual licence – entry for a payment e.g. buying a ticket for a rugby match (*The Rugby Football Union v Viagogo Ltd* [2011]).

- A licence may be withdrawn and the visitor will become a trespasser if they do not leave within a reasonable period of being asked to leave the premises.

## 9.3.2 Necessity

- This defence is available if there is an immediate danger to life or property and the defendant acts reasonably in the circumstances.

| Case: | |
|---|---|
| ***Esso v Southport Corporation* [1956]** | An Esso tanker ran aground without negligence. The tanker was in danger of breaking up and the captain discharged oil to refloat it. The oil fouled the Corporation's beach and they sued for trespass. It was held that the captain had acted to save lives and necessity was a good defence. |

- The defence of necessity is quite narrow as seen in the following case.

| Case: | |
|---|---|
| *Monsanto v Tilly* **(1999)** | The claimant was growing some genetically modified crops. The defendants believed that the crops were a danger to the public and pulled up some of the plants. The court said that the defendants had acted to gain publicity and there was no immediate danger to the public. Therefore it was trespass to land. |

## 9.3.3 Lawful justification

- A number of statutes give authority to certain persons to enter the claimant's land e.g. Police and Criminal Evidence Act 1984 gives a police officer power to enter premises and search them or for the purpose of making an arrest.

# 9.4 Remedies

- The most important remedies are **damages** and **injunctions** (see Chapter 15). The following are additional remedies.

## 9.4.1 Self-help

- A person in possession of land may use reasonable force to stop entry by a trespasser or to evict a trespasser from land.

## 9.4.2 Action for possession

- A person who has lost possession of land may obtain a court order to regain possession.

| Checkpoint – trespass to land: defences and remedies | |
|---|---|
| **Task** | **Done** |
| I can explain the nature and effect of a licence for land | |
| I understand the defence of necessity and the limits of that defence | |
| I can state four remedies available for trespass to land | |

## Research Point

Look up the following extract: Harlow, C. (2005) *Understanding Tort Law*, (3rd edn, Ch 5, pp 79–82, London: Thomson, Sweet & Maxwell).

Explain how injunctions are used between neighbours in cases of trespass and nuisance, giving examples to illustrate your answer.

## Potential exam question

Joe bought a ticket to watch his local amateur football team, Rovers FC. On the ticket it stated 'No one may use any recording equipment in the stadium'. While Joe was at the match he started using his video camera to record parts of the game. Kamran, a club steward, saw Joe doing this and asked him to leave the stadium.

During the game Len, a Rovers player, accidentally kicked the ball over a wall and it landed in the garden of a house which backed on to the stadium. Mary is the tenant of the house. Nick, a ball boy, climbed over the wall to retrieve the ball.

In the second half of the match the weather turned windy. A hot air balloon, piloted by Olive, which was travelling near the stadium, was blown over the pitch.

Rovers FC lost the game 4–0. A crowd of 50 supporters gathered on the public road outside the club offices chanting for the manager to resign.

Advise (i) Joe, (ii) Len, (iii) Nick, (iv) Olive and (v) the supporters of their liability, if any, for trespass to land.

# Chapter 10

## Occupiers' Liability

## 10.1 Introduction

- The tort of occupiers' liability deals with the liability of the occupier of premises to those who come on to the premises. The rules were originally developed by the common law but the above two statutes were passed to clarify the law and they set out more detailed rules.

### 10.1.1 Common law

- At common law entrants to land were divided into four categories and the duty owed to them became progressively less.

| Contractual visitor | duty to see premises were safe e.g. paying customer at a swimming pool |
|---|---|
| Invitee | duty to prevent damage from an unusual danger e.g. customer in a shop |
| Licensee | duty to protect from concealed danger e.g. asking a friend to visit your house |
| Trespasser | duty not to intentionally or recklessly harm e.g. someone climbs into your garden over your garden wall |

- The above rules were set out in *Addie & Sons v Dumbreck* [1929]. In *British Railway Board v Herrington* [1972] the House of Lords said that trespassers were owed a 'duty of common humanity' which was a minimum level.

- The common law rules are still relevant as s1 Occupiers' Liability Act (OLA) 1957 says that visitors are those who were invitees or licensees.

- Also if an entrant falls outside the requirements of either of the two OLAs then the common law rules apply.

# 10.2 Occupiers' Liability Act 1957

## 10.2.1 What does the duty under the OLA 1957 cover?

- OLA 1957 covers:

  1. personal injury

  2. death

  3. damage to property.

## 10.2.2 What does 'premises' cover?

- OLA 1957 s1(3)(a) provides that the Act covers 'the obligations of a person occupying or having control over any fixed or movable structure including any vessel, vehicle or aircraft'. This has even been held to apply to a ladder, *Wheeler v Copas* [1981].

## 10.2.3 Who is an occupier?

- The OLA 1957 does not define occupier but says that the common law rules apply.

- *Wheat v Lacon* [1966] provided that an occupier has some degree of control over premises. In that case both the owner and manager of a public house were held to be the 'occupiers'.

- **Point to note:** there may be more than one occupier.

- There is no need to have physical possession of the premises, the legal **right of control** can make someone an occupier.

| Case: | |
|---|---|
| *Harris v Birkenhead Corporation* **[1976]** | The corporation put a compulsory purchase order on a house but did not take possession of it. A four-year-old child went into the house, fell out of a window and was injured. It was held that the corporation were liable as occupiers. |

## 10.2.4 Who is a visitor?

- A visitor is anyone with:

  - **express** permission to be on the premises.

    This permission may be limited by the area they can go into, the purpose of their visit and the time they are on the premises. If a visitor goes outside these limits they may become a trespasser.

  - **implied** permission e.g. a postman.

  - a **legal right** to enter e.g. a fire officer putting out a fire; a police officer with a search warrant s2(6) OLA 1957.

- Note that someone using a **public right of way** is not a visitor under the OLA 1957, neither are they covered by the OLA 1984. The only rights they have are at common law.

## 10.2.5 What duty is owed under the OLA 1957?

- Under s2(1) an occupier owes **the common duty of care** to all his visitors. This is a duty to take such care as in all the circumstances is reasonable to see that the visitor is reasonably safe in using the premises for the purposes he is invited.

- **Point to note:** It is the visitor not the premises that must be safe.

- In determining this duty the courts take into account the same factors as a claim in negligence e.g. the risk of harm.

- But note that under s2(1) the occupier can extend, restrict, modify or exclude his duty.

# 10.3 Special Categories of Visitor

- The duty varies according to who the visitor is.

| Children | Specialists | Independent contractors |
|---|---|---|
| Higher duty owed because they take less care than adults | Duty owed to them but not for the normal risks of their job | Occupier not liable for acts of contractor if three checks satisfactorily completed |

## 10.3.1 Children

*'An occupier must be prepared for children to be less careful than adults'. (s2(3))*

- The courts have long accepted that more care must be taken by the occupier when dealing with children. Many ordinary things may appear attractive to children and can act as 'allurements'. The occupier must take this into account as seen in the next case.

- Even before the OLA 1957 the courts accepted that the standard of care expected with children was higher.

| Case: | |
|---|---|
| **Glasgow Corporation v Taylor [1922]** | A seven-year-old child picked some poisonous red berries from a bush in a public park, ate them and died. It was held that the defendants were liable as no warning was given and the berries were an allurement and turned the child trespasser into an implied visitor. |

- If children are very young then the occupier can expect the parents to have the primary responsibility for them. It does not take away the occupiers' responsibility entirely. The courts will take into account the nature of the danger and the age of the child.

| Case: | |
|---|---|
| **Phipps v Rochester Corporation [1955]** | A seven-year-old girl and her five-year-old brother went blackberry picking on the defendant's building site. The boy fell into a trench and broke his leg. Held that the defendants were not liable as the main responsibility for young children is with their parents. |

- This principle was followed in *Bourne Leisure Ltd v Marsden* [2009].

| Case: | |
|---|---|
| **Bourne Leisure Ltd v Marsden [2009]** | A two-year-old boy wandered off from his mother and drowned in a pond on a holiday park. The CA said that the holiday park was not liable because there was no duty to fence all such ponds and it could expect parents to supervise the child. |

- The House of Lords has stated that the ingenuity of children in finding ways to do mischief should not be underestimated. In *Jolley v Sutton*

*LBC* [2000] a 14-year-old boy propped up an abandoned boat on his housing estate to try and fix it but was injured when the boat fell on him. The House of Lords found the defendant council liable under the OLA 1957 as it was foreseeable children would meddle with the boat.

## 10.3.2 Specialists

*'An occupier can expect that a **specialist** with a skill will guard against the ordinary risks of their job'.* (s2(3)(b))

- For example, if a roofer falls off a roof and injures themselves because they overbalance, the occupier is not liable.

- Note that the occupier does owe a duty to specialists but not in respect of the normal risks of their job e.g. occupier liable to a post office engineer who fell through a defective skylight on the roof.

## 10.3.3 Independent contractors

- Section 2(4)(b) OLA provides that the occupier is **not** liable for damage caused to a visitor due to faulty execution of work of construction, maintenance or repair by an independent contractor, if the occupier:

1. **Acted reasonably** in giving the work to the contractor. It is reasonable to give skilled and technical work to an expert and may be industry practice to give basic work to a contractor e.g. cleaning.

2. Took reasonable steps to **check that the contractor was competent**. This may involve checking **the contractor is a member of a trade association**, etc.

3. **Checked that the work** was completed properly. It would be unreasonable to expect the occupier to check technical work but in *Haseldine* (below) the occupier could check that the lift worked. An occupier would be expected to check a simple matter such as steps had been cleared of ice (*Woodward v Mayor of Hastings* [1945]).

| Case: | |
|---|---|
| ***Haseldine v Daw* [1941]** | The defendant owned a block of flats and engaged a competent firm of engineers to service the lift. Shortly after this the claimant was injured when the lift fell to the bottom of the lift shaft. It was held that the defendant was not liable as it was reasonable to employ a specialist. |

### Workpoint

Alice took her little boy Ben, aged 3, to the park which was owned by Wessex Council. While Ben was playing Alice started to read a book. Ben wandered off and fell into the boating lake and was injured.

Dave, a fencing contractor, was taken on by Wessex Council to replace the old railings around the park which were rusting and had been damaged by vandals. Dave started work but was injured when a section of the railings fell over and cut him.

Eddie, a contractor, was taken on by Wessex Council to instal showers in the tennis changing rooms. A week after the work was finished Fiona was having a shower when the shower fitting fell on her and injured her shoulder.

Advise Wessex Council whether it owes a duty of care under the OLA 1957 to Ben, Dave and Fiona and if so, whether it is in breach of duty.

# 10.4 Defences

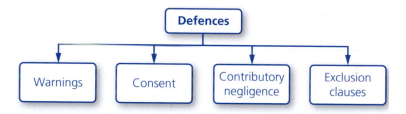

### 10.4.1 Warnings

- Section 2(4)(a) provides that if damage is caused by something which the visitor has been warned about, that is not enough to avoid liability by the occupier unless the warning was enough to enable the visitor to be reasonably safe. In *Roles v Nathan* [1963](CA) Lord Denning gave the following example to illustrate how s2(4) would work.

- If the only way into premises was a rotten footbridge over a stream and the occupier put up a notice 'This bridge is dangerous', then under s2(4) the occupier would be liable if the visitor was injured using the bridge.

- If there were two footbridges, a rotten one and a safe one, the occupier could put up a notice, 'Do not use this footbridge. It is dangerous. There is a safe one further up stream'. This warning enables the visitor to be safe and the occupier would not be liable if the visitor used the rotten bridge and suffered injury.

- In deciding whether the warning is sufficient the courts will take into account many factors such as:

  - Is the warning sign large enough?

  - Is it in a prominent place?

  - Does it specify what the danger is? (*Rae v Mars Ltd* [1990])

  - How old is the visitor – can they read?

  - Is a warning enough or is the danger so great that a barrier is needed?

  - Is the danger obvious? (*Staples v West Dorset DC* [1995](CA))

- Note in *Rae v Mars* [1990] a surveyor entered an unlit storeroom and fell down a one-metre drop from the doorway and broke his ankle. It was held that because of the exceptional nature of this danger he should have been given a specific warning. This was a breach of the common duty of care under s2 OLA 1957. However, because he did not switch on his torch the claimant's damages were reduced by one third for contributory negligence.

## 10.4.2 Consent

- Section 2(5) provides that the occupier is not liable for risks which the visitor willingly accepts.

- The visitor must have a real choice about taking the risk.

## 10.4.3 Contributory negligence

- Section 2(3) provides that in determining the common duty of care the degree of care and want of care of the visitor is taken into account. If the visitor is partly to blame for the damage then the court may reduce the damages payable under the Law Reform (Contributory Negligence) Act 1945.

## 10.4.4 Exclusion clauses

- Section 2(1) provides that the occupier may 'restrict, modify or exclude' the common duty of care to the extent that the law allows.

- However, any notice excluding liability is subject to the Unfair Contract Terms Act (UCTA) 1977:

  - Any attempt to exclude liability for **death or injury** arising from negligence in the course of a business is void (s2(1) of UCTA).

- Any attempt to exclude liability for other loss or damage is subject to a test of reasonableness (S2(2) of UCTA).

- A business occupier is subject to UCTA but a private occupier is not.

- It is important to distinguish between a **warning notice** and an **exclusion** clause as any attempt to exclude liability is subject to UCTA 1977.

## Checkpoint – OLA 1957

| Task | Done |
|---|---|
| I can explain what is needed to be an occupier | |
| I can define the common duty of care owed under the OLA 1957 | |
| I can explain the duty the occupier owes to children | |
| I can explain when an independent contractor will be liable instead of the occupier | |
| I can identify four defences available to an occupier | |

## Research Point

Look up the following article: Wake, P. (2010) Personal injury: Sense & sensibility, 160 *NLJ* 931. In *Esdale v Dover District Council* [2010] EWCA Civ 409 Mrs Esdale appealed to the Court of Appeal on the basis that the council had not followed its own policy to repair defects of more than three quarters of an inch and was therefore in breach of the common duty of care.

Explain the decision of the Court of Appeal and the reason for that decision.

# 10.5 Occupiers' Liability Act 1984

- The original common law rule was that no duty was owed to trespassers as long as the occupier did not intentionally harm them. The OLA 1957 does not cover trespassers. Before the OLA 1984 was passed the courts gave trespassers some protection by developing the concept of the 'implied visitor'.

| Case: | |
|---|---|
| *British Railways Board v Herrington* [1972] | A six-year-old boy climbed through a broken fence on to an electrified railway line and was burned. The railway knew that this route was used as a shortcut. It was held by HL that the defendant owed a duty of common humanity to the boy and was liable. |

- **Point to note:** if someone is not covered under either the OLA 1957 or the OLA 1984 they may still be owed a duty of common humanity (at common law).

- Who does the OLA 1984 apply to?

  - trespassers

  - people using private rights of way

  - people exercising rights under the National Parks and Access to the Countryside Act 1949 and the Countryside and Rights of Way Act 2000.

- Note that the OLA 1984 does not apply to someone using a **public right of way** so only the common law rules apply in that case.

- What does the duty cover?

  - s1(1) a duty is owed for **injury** due to the state of the premises or things done or omitted to be done on them.

  - s1(8) no liability for loss or damage to **property**.

## 10.5.1 Who is an occupier?

- An occupier is someone with a sufficient degree of control over the land. The fact someone has access to land does not give them sufficient control (*Bailey v Armes* [1999]).

## 10.5.2 When is a duty owed under the Act?

- The OLA 1984 does not use the word 'trespasser' but persons 'other than visitors'. This covers a wider group than trespassers but the main category will be trespassers.

- Section 1(3) a duty is owed when the occupier:

  1. is aware of the danger or has reasonable grounds to know about it, and

2. knows or has reasonable grounds to believe someone is near the danger, and

3. the risk is one which in all the circumstances the trespasser should be protected from.

• How these factors apply can be seen in the following cases:

| Case: | |
|---|---|
| **Ratcliff v McConnell [1998]** | The defendants owned a college with an outdoor swimming pool. A notice on the gate stated that the pool must not be used between 10.00pm and 6.30am. At the end of the day the pool was locked. The claimant was a 19-year-old student at the college. Early one morning, in winter, he climbed over the gates and dived into the pool. The water was shallow and he hit his head on the bottom of the pool and was badly injured. It was held that the defendants knew of the danger, the pool. But even if they knew students climbed over the gates they did not have to warn them of the danger, diving into the pool at night, because that was obvious to an adult. The defendants were not liable. |

| Case: | |
|---|---|
| **Tomlinson v Congleton BC & Another [2003]** | The defendants owned a country park with a lake. A notice stated, 'Dangerous water: no swimming'. The claimant, aged 18, was standing in the lake with the water below his knees and dived in. He struck his head on the bottom and was paralysed. It was held that the risk was from the claimant's own act, diving into shallow water and not from the state of the premises. The defendants were not liable. |

• In the House of Lords Lord Hoffmann in applying s1(3) said that (a) the occupier was aware of the danger to anyone diving in the lake; (b) the occupier knew that people were near the lake; and (c) was the risk one which the occupier should have offered some protection from – the answer was no because the danger of diving in shallow water was obvious.

| Case: | |
|-------|--|
| **Keown v Coventry Healthcare NHS Trust [2006]** | An 11-year-old boy went into the grounds of a hospital, climbed on to an outside fire escape and fell 10 metres to the ground. He was badly injured. The hospital knew that the public used the grounds as a shortcut and that children played in the grounds. The county court found the defendants liable. The Court of Appeal found that the boy admitted he should not have been climbing the fire escape. It held that the injury was not due to the state of the premises and the defendants were not liable. Otherwise the defendants would have to cordon off trees, drain pipes, etc. |

- In determining if the occupier has taken reasonable care under (c) a number of factors are taken into account. These include:

1. whether the entry was accidental or intentional

2. the nature of the risk

3. the age of the trespasser

4. the cost of precautions etc.

## Research Point

Look up the case of *Harvey v Plymouth City Council* [2010] EWCA Civ 860 and also look up Harris, J, (2010), Personal injury: Keep out, 160 NLJ 1339.

Explain the status of the claimant and the decision at first instance. Explain the status of the claimant and the decision in the Court of Appeal.

Look up the following article: Macleod, R. (2010), Personal Injury/ Occupiers' Liability: What do you mean it's my fault? 160 *NLJ* 567.

1) Explain the cases of:

   *Paul Mann v Northern Electric Distribution Ltd* [2010],
   *Gary Poppleton v Trustees of the Portsmouth Youth Activities Committee* [2008], and *Uren v Corporate Leisure (UK) Ltd* [2010].

2) Explain the overall effect of such decisions.

*OCCUPIERS' LIABILITY*

# 10.6 Defences

| Warnings | Consent | Exclusion clauses |
|----------|---------|-------------------|
| The occupier may discharge his duty by 'taking such steps as are reasonable in all the circumstances' to warn of the danger s1(5). | The occupier is not liable for any risks 'willingly accepted' s1(6). | There is no provision under the OLA 1984 to exclude liability.<br><br>The UCTA 1977 does not apply to the OLA 1984. |
| The warning must take into account: the nature of the danger; the age of the trespasser; etc. | In *Ratcliff v McConnell* [1998] the 19-year-old claimant accepted the risks. | The result is that a trespasser could be in a better position than a visitor because the occupier cannot exclude liability. |

| Case: | |
|-------|--|
| ***Geary v JD Weatherspoon* [2011]** | The claimant went to a bar on the first floor of the defendant's public house for some drinks with her workmates. The building had a grand staircase with banisters (stair rails). When the claimant was leaving she climbed onto the banisters intending to slide down but she fell four metres onto the marble floor. As a result she injured her spine and was paralysed. She sued in negligence but the court accepted that the claim could equally have been under the Occupiers' Liability Acts. The defendants had put down some mats and warned people not to slide down the banisters although they had not put up a warning sign. It was held that the defendant owed no duty to protect the claimant from such an obvious risk and the claimant had voluntarily taken the risk of injury. The claim failed. |

## Checkpoint – OLA 1984

| Task | Done |
|------|------|
| I understand when the duty of common humanity would apply | |
| I can explain the categories of people protected by the OLA 1984 | |
| I can identify and explain the three requirements for a duty to be owed under the OLA 1984 | |
| I can explain the decision in *Keown v Coventry Healthcare NHS Trust* (2006) | |
| I understand the requirements for a warning to be valid under the OLA 1984 | |

## Potential exam question

Use the knowledge and understanding you have of the OLA 1957 and OLA 1984 to outline an answer to the following question.

Remember to consider whether someone is a visitor and if not whether they are a trespasser.

Donna took her son Fred, aged 10, for a week's holiday at a holiday camp owned by Happy Hols. The holiday camp overlooked the sea.

On the first day Fred went for a swim in the children's swimming pool. He jumped into the pool and cut his foot on a broken glass bottle at the bottom of the pool. The pool had been cleaned the previous day by George, a local swimming pool cleaning specialist. Happy Hols had chosen George after seeing his advertisement in the local newspaper.

On the second day, while Fred was at a children's activity class, Donna went for a walk along the cliff path which ran through the holiday camp. Happy Hols had put up a notice saying 'Warning – Dangerous Cliffs'. Donna was walking along the path when she tripped in a pothole on the path. She put out her hands to break her fall but broke two fingers when she hit the ground.

On the third day, Ivy, aged 13, who lived near the holiday camp, wandered into the camp and started to climb a tree. She had

*Continued overleaf*

climbed about five metres from the ground when she slipped and fell, breaking her leg. Her new jeans were also badly torn in the fall. The security guards at the holiday camp had seen local teenagers climbing trees on several occasions and had chased them away.

Advise (i) Fred, (ii) Donna and (iii) Ivy of the claims they may make, if any, under the Occupiers' Liability Acts.

# Chapter 11

## Trespass to the person

## 11.1 Introduction

- This chapter will explain trespass to the person which consists of the torts of assault, battery and false imprisonment and it will also explain the tort of *Wilkinson v Downton* and the tort of harassment.

```
                    ┌─────────────────────────┐
                    │  Trespass to the person │
                    └─────────────────────────┘
          ┌──────────────────┼──────────────────────┐
┌──────────────────┐  ┌──────────────────┐  ┌──────────────────────┐
│     Assault      │  │     Battery      │  │  False imprisonment  │
└──────────────────┘  └──────────────────┘  └──────────────────────┘
```

- To be a trespass to the person the act must be **direct**.

- A **direct act** is an act which directly affects the other person, e.g throwing a stick at them.

- An **indirect act** is an act which affects them but not in such a direct way, e.g. throwing a stick in the road and the other person trips over it. In this case the claim is in negligence.

| Case: | |
|---|---|
| ***Letang v Cooper* [1965]** | The claimant was sunbathing on the grass in a hotel car park when the defendant negligently drove his car over her legs. More than three years later she sued. Under the Limitation Acts a claim in negligence is barred three years after the accident but a claim in trespass may be made up to six years afterwards. The claimant sued for trespass. The Court of Appeal said that if force is intentionally applied directly to another, a claim may be made in trespass to the person. If an injury is caused unintentionally the claim is only in negligence. Here the injury was unintentional and the claimant's claim was in negligence but it was barred under the Limitation Acts and failed. |

- Another distinction from a claim in negligence is that each of the torts of assault, battery and false imprisonment are actionable *per se* (in itself). This means that a claim may be made even if no harm is caused.

# 11.2 Assault

> **Definition**
>
> Assault: an act which causes another person to apprehend the infliction of immediate, unlawful, force on his person. (Goff LJ in *Collins v Wilcock* [1984])

- The word 'assault' therefore has a particular meaning in trespass which is not the everyday meaning of the word which is hitting someone. The legal meaning is that someone is subjected to a threat of immediate harm.

- For example, raising a fist to someone would make them believe that you were going to hit them.

| Case: | |
|---|---|
| ***Stephens v Myers* (1830)** | A group of people were sitting round a table at a parish meeting. Following an argument the defendant stood up and with his fist clenched moved towards the claimant. He was stopped from reaching him by someone else. It was held that even though he was not near enough to hit the claimant, the claimant had been put in fear of being hit and this was an assault. |

- The threat must put the claimant in fear of an **immediate** battery.

| Case: | |
|---|---|
| ***Thomas v National Union of Mineworkers* [1985]** | Striking miners formed pickets outside the mine. As the working miners were taken into the mine by bus large numbers of striking miners shouted threats at them. The striking miners were held back by the police. It was held that the miners on the bus were safe and there was no danger of an immediate battery, so that no assault had been committed. |

- Can words alone be an assault? There are conflicting cases on this point.

  - *Meade's Case* (1823) it was said that words were not an assault.

  - *R v Wilson* [1955] the court said that words could be an assault.

- In *R v Ireland* [1998] the House of Lords said that silent phone calls were an assault and the court doubted *Meade's Case* and said that words could amount to an assault.

- Words may be relevant in deciding whether an act amounts to an assault.

| Case: | |
|---|---|
| **Tuberville v Savage (1669)** | The defendant put his hand on his sword and said, 'If it were not Assize time I would not take such language from you'. The Assizes were judges travelling around trying cases. The defendant was effectively saying that because the judges were in town he was not going to do anything. Putting his hand on his sword would usually be seen as an assault but the words meant there was no assault. It was held that this was not an assault. |

- **Point to note:** For an assault to take place there is no need for any physical contact.

## Checkpoint – assault

| Task | Done |
|---|---|
| I can define assault | |
| I can explain the need for fear of an immediate battery | |
| I can explain how words may be relevant to assault | |
| I can explain the effect of the words in *Tuberville v Savage* (1669) | |

# 11.3 Battery

## Definition

Battery: the direct application of unlawful force to another person, e.g. punching someone.

- There does not have to be personal contact, for example, by touching someone with your hand.

  - Throwing water over someone would be a battery.

  - Snatching a handbag from someone would be a battery.

## 11.3.1 Force

- There is no need for the act to be with force. 'The least touching of another in anger is a battery' (*Cole v Turner* (1704)). The purpose of the tort of trespass is not only to protect someone from physical harm but to protect their 'personal integrity' which means that people must be left alone.

## 11.3.2 Intention to apply force

- The defendant must intend to do the act. If the act is merely done negligently then the claim must be in negligence and not trespass to the person (see *Letang v Cooper* at 11.1).

- There is no need for an intention to cause harm.

- Some physical contact is accepted as part of everyday life e.g. jostling with other people in a crowded street or giving someone a friendly slap on the back. Such actions would not be battery.

- One problem issue is whether the act has to be done with a 'hostile' intent.

| Case: | |
|---|---|
| ***Wilson v Pringle* [1986]** | The claimant and defendant were both 13-year-old schoolboys. The claimant was walking along a corridor with his bag over his shoulder. The defendant pulled the bag off his shoulder causing him to fall to the ground and injure his hip. The defendant argued that this was merely horseplay and not a battery. The High Court decided that this was a battery. The Court of Appeal said that the touching must be hostile and therefore it was not a battery. |

- What exactly does 'hostile' mean? In *Wilson v Pringle* the court gave some examples like punching, stabbing and shooting. It also gave the following criminal case as an example.

| Case: | |
|---|---|
| *Collins v Wilcock* [1984] | W, a police officer on duty in the street suspected C of soliciting. The officer tried to question C but she walked away. W then took hold of her arm and C scratched the officer. C was subsequently convicted of criminal assault. On appeal the court said that when the officer took hold of her arm the officer was not arresting C. The act was beyond acceptable physical contact between two citizens. It was unlawful, hostile and therefore a battery by W. C's conviction was quashed. |

- In *Re F* [1990] Lord Goff in the House of Lords doubted whether the touching had to be hostile for the purposes of battery:

*'I respectfully doubt whether that is correct. A prank that gets out of hand; an overfriendly slap on the back; surgical treatment by a surgeon who mistakenly thinks the patient has consented to it – all these things may transcend the bounds of lawfulness, without being characterised as hostile. Indeed the suggested qualification is difficult to reconcile with the principle that any touching of another's body is, in the absence of a lawful excuse, capable of amounting to a battery and a trespass.'*

- This leaves the law uncertain about the requirement that the act be 'hostile'.

- One further point on intent is that it only needs to be proved that the defendant intended to apply force to **another person**. It does not matter that the person hit was not the intended victim. The principle of 'transferred intent' from criminal law applies.

| Case: | |
|---|---|
| *Livingstone v Ministry of Defence* [1984] | A soldier fired a rubber bullet at a rioter but missed and hit the claimant by mistake. The defendant argued that it was not battery because he did not intend to hit the claimant. The soldier was liable in battery. |

- **Point to note:** Assault and battery usually occur together as the victim will see the other person raise a fist or a stick. But if the victim is hit from behind it will only be a battery.

Workpoint

A opens his bedroom window on the first floor of his terraced house and sees B walking past. A raises his fist and shouts that he will thump B.

C is driving his car through the town centre when a crowd of people block the road, surrounding his car. D bangs on the roof with a stick. C manages to drive away without coming to any harm.

E is walking through a busy shop one weekend when F, who is walking in the opposite direction, collides with E.

G threw a tennis ball to his friend H but missed and hit I.

Explain whether any tort has been committed in each of the above situations.

## Checkpoint – battery

| Task | Done |
|---|---|
| I can define battery | |
| I can explain the purpose of the law of battery is not only protection from physical harm | |
| I can explain the two sides of the argument about hostile intent | |
| I understand the effect of *Wilson v Pringle* (1986) | |
| I can apply the principle of transferred intent | |

# 11.4 False imprisonment

## Definition

False imprisonment: stopping someone moving freely without a lawful justification.

## 11.4.1 Must be restraint

- False imprisonment is committed if there is any act which prevents freedom of movement. It does not require that someone is imprisoned or is physically restrained.

- For example, a teacher telling a pupil to wait in a room. Merely blocking someone's way is not false imprisonment.

## 11.4.2 The restraint must be total

- To be false imprisonment there must be no reasonable way out.

| Case: | |
|---|---|
| **Bird v Jones (1845)** | The defendant fenced off part of the footpath on Hammersmith Bridge for people to pay to watch a rowing race. The claimant, who usually walked along the footpath, climbed over the fence without paying but was stopped from walking further through the fenced off part, by two police officers. He could have gone back and crossed the bridge on the other side. It was held that he had not been falsely imprisoned because he had a way out. The court said that a prison must have a boundary. |

- In *Bird v Jones* the claimant had a reasonable way out. If someone was locked in a ground floor room it may be reasonable for them to climb out of a window but if the room was on the first floor then it would not be reasonable to expect them to climb out of the window unless they were particularly athletic!

- Originally a person had to know that they had been restrained to claim false imprisonment. In *Herring v Boyle* (1834) a boy kept at boarding school during the Christmas holidays because his mother had not paid the fees was not falsely imprisoned because he did not realise. This principle was doubted in the next case.

| Case: | |
|---|---|
| **Meering v Grahame-White Aviation Ltd [1919]** | The claimant was suspected of theft by his employer and was asked to go to a room to answer some questions. He was in the room for an hour. Unknown to him two works police officers were outside the door and had been told not to let him leave until the police arrived. It was held that he had been falsely imprisoned. Atkin LJ said that a person could be imprisoned if he was asleep, drunk or unconscious. |

- The House of Lords confirmed in *Murray v Ministry of Defence* [1988] that a person can be falsely imprisoned without knowing that they are.

- **Point to note:** The defendant may have a defence of lawful arrest.

### Checkpoint – false imprisonment

| Task | Done |
|------|------|
| I can define false imprisonment | |
| I can explain the requirement for total restraint | |
| I understand the effect of *Meering v Grahame-White Aviation* (1919) | |

# 11.5 Defences

## 11.5.1 Consent

- If someone consents to a battery this will be a good defence. Examples include consenting to medical treatment and playing contact sports like football.

- The consent may be given expressly, for example, signing a form for an operation. Or it may be implied, for example, playing in a game of football or hockey means consenting to the risks of the game.

| Case: | |
|-------|---|
| ***Herd v Weardale Steel Co*** **[1915]** | The claimant miner went down the mine for his shift. He was asked to do work he believed was dangerous but refused and asked to be taken to the surface. Although the lift was available he was kept down the mine for 20 minutes. He sued for false imprisonment. It was held by the House of Lords that the claimant had consented to go down the mine and under his contract had no right to come up until the end of his shift. This was not false imprisonment. |

## 11.5.2 Self-defence

- A person may use 'reasonable force' to defend themselves or another person from attack. The burden is on the defendant to prove that the force used was 'reasonable'.

| Case: | |
|---|---|
| **Lane v Holloway** **[1968]** | The claimant (aged 64) returned from the pub, stopped outside his door and started chatting to a neighbour. The defendant's wife, who lived next door, called out to him. The claimant replied, 'Shut up you monkey-faced tart'. The defendant (aged 23) then appeared and the claimant said 'I want to see you on your own'. The defendant went up to the claimant who punched him on the shoulder. The defendant then punched the claimant once in the face. The cut needed 19 stitches. It was held that the defendant's act was out of all proportion in these circumstances and he could not claim self-defence. The claimant had not consented to such a savage injury by taking part in a fight. |

## 11.5.3 Lawful arrest

- The police have certain powers of arrest both at common law and under statute. If they use these powers according to the rules they may lawfully commit assault, battery and false imprisonment. The main statute is the Police and Criminal Evidence Act 1984 (as amended).

- **Point to note:** The defence of **contributory negligence** is not available in intentional torts like trespass to the person and the Law Reform (Contributory Negligence) Act 1945 does not apply (*Co-operative Group Ltd v Pritchard* [2011] (CA)).

### Workpoint

J went to K's fairground. J paid £5 to go on a trip on the ghost train. Each trip consisted of two circuits of the track. After the first circuit the train arrived at the station and J wanted to get off but K refused to let him. J had to go round again.

Advise J if he has a claim for false imprisonment.

**Checkpoint – defences**

| Task | Done |
|------|------|
| I can explain the defence of consent and give examples. | |
| I can explain *Herd v Weardale Steel Co* (1915). | |
| I understand the requirement for 'reasonable force' in self defence. | |

# 11.6 Tort of *Wilkinson v Downton*

• The rule in *Wilkinson v Downton* is usually explained alongside trespass to the person because like trespass it is an intentional tort. It addresses the intentional infliction of emotional distress.

| Case: | |
|-------|--|
| ***Wilkinson v Downton* [1897]** | The defendant, as a joke, told the claimant that her husband had broken both his legs. The claimant went off to find her husband and suffered psychiatric injury (nervous shock) and became physically ill. The court held that if someone intentionally does an act calculated to cause physical harm they are legally liable. Therefore the defendant was liable. |

• At the time of the case no claims were allowed in negligence for **psychiatric injury** (nervous shock). Neither could the claimant sue for **trespass to the person**, as the defendant did not threaten or touch her.

| Case: | |
|---|---|
| **Wainwright v Home Office [2003]** | A mother and one of her sons went to visit another son who was in prison. Because of the problem of drugs being taken into prison they were both strip-searched. Although they consented this consent was invalid because the search was in breach of prison rules. As a result of this experience the mother suffered distress and her son suffered shaking. They claimed on the basis of *Wilkinson v Downton*. It was held by the House of Lords that *Wilkinson v Downton* did not provide a remedy if the distress did not amount to a recognised psychiatric injury and their claims failed. |

- Note that the son's claim for **battery** succeeded in the Court of Appeal.

- To bring a claim within the rule in *Wilkinson v Downton* there must be an intention to cause harm and this must result in physical harm or a recognised psychiatric harm.

- Only one single act of harassment is needed and this distinguishes such a claim from one under the **Protection from Harassment Act 1997.**

# 11.7 Harassment

- The **Protection from Harassment Act 1997** creates criminal offences dealing with harassment. If harassment is proved the Act also provides a right to sue in tort for damages and/or obtain an injunction (s3).

- The Act does not define 'harassment' but under s1 there must be a 'course of conduct'. This is further defined in s7(3) to mean conduct on at least two occasions. This is an important distinction from *Wilkinson v Downton* [1897] when one act is sufficient.

- The Act provides a remedy in cases of stalking, sending text messages, etc.

| Case: | |
|---|---|
| *Ferguson v British Gas* **[2009]** | The claimant had been a customer of the defendant but changed to a new supplier. She continued to receive bills and letters threatening to cut off her gas supply even after she had complained about this. The Court of Appeal said that this amounted to harassment. The conduct was sufficiently grave. The defendant's argument that the letters were generated by computer carried no weight as they were read by a real person. |

## Potential exam question

Ray, a sixth-form student, went to London to protest about the increase in tuition fees. As he walked towards the Houses of Parliament he was confronted by Sophie, a police officer. She raised her baton and told Ray to stop. Ray, believing that he was about to be hit, punched Sophie in the face and ran off.

Tina, a university student, was in the crowd of protestors outside Parliament. As a car carrying Ugo, a Member of Parliament, drove slowly through the crowd Tina banged a stick against the car window and shouted, 'I'm going to kill you!' at Ugo.

Vida, a 60-year-old university lecturer, who was on the demonstration went into an office building with a number of other demonstrators. Willy, a well-built 20-year-old man, who was working in the building, grabbed Vida by the arm. In response Vida slapped him. Willy pushed her to the ground breaking two of her ribs. He then took Vida to a first floor room and locked her in saying that he was calling the police. Vida was in the room for about 20 minutes before other demonstrators broke down the door and rescued her.

Advise (i) Ray, (ii) Sophie, (iii) Ugo, (iv) Vida and (v) Willy of any claims they may bring in tort in respect of the above incidents.

# Chapter 12
# Vicarious liability

## 12.1 Introduction

> **Definition**
>
> Vicarious liability: the rule that one person is liable in tort for the actions of another.

- For example, an employer is liable for a tort committed by an employee.

- **Point to Note:** Vicarious liability is not a tort.

- The employer is vicariously liable but the employee is also directly liable for their tort. However, in practice, an employee would only be held liable if they committed a deliberate act.

- There are three requirements for vicarious liability to arise:

**3 requirements for vicarious liability**

| Tort must be committed | Must be committed by employee | Must be in the course of employment |

## 12.1.1 A tort must be committed
- It must be established that the employee has committed a **tort**. If this cannot be established then the employer is not vicariously liable.

## 12.1.2 It must be committed by an employee
- The law makes a distinction between **employees** and **independent contractors**. The employer is only liable for the torts of an employee not those of an independent contractor.

- For example, an office worker or a teacher will be employees.

- A plumber or a barrister will be independent contractors.

- This distinction is not as clear-cut as it used to be. Many people now work for themselves as independent contractors but may spend a good deal of time working for one company. Do they become employees?

- The courts have developed various tests to help to decide whether someone is an employee or an independent contractor.

### 12.1.2.1 The control test

- If one person has control over the other and tells them what to do and how to do it, then the other person is an employee.

- This test was widely used when most people were unskilled. It is of less importance in an educated and technological society where people are unlikely to be told how to do their jobs.

- The control test is still used but is not enough on its own to determine who is an employee.

### 12.1.2.2 The organisation test (or integration test)

- Is the person integrated into the business organisation or only an accessory to it, i.e. are they 'part and parcel' of the organisation?

- For example, a surgeon in a hospital is integrated into the organisation and therefore an employee.

- This test was of limited use as it was difficult to apply in practice.

### 12.1.2.3 The economic reality test

- This test, which is also known as the multiple test, was developed in the following case. This is the test which is usually used by the courts.

| Case: | |
|---|---|
| ***Ready Mixed Concrete v Minister of Pensions and National Insurance* [1968]** | RMC delivered concrete. The drivers were described as self-employed, they were paid a fixed rate per mile, they had to buy the lorries on hire purchase, drivers had to maintain and insure the lorries, the lorries had to be in the company colours, drivers had to wear a uniform and be available when required. Were the drivers employees or independent contractors? It was held, applying the economic reality test, that ownership of the lorries and taking the risk of loss pointed to the drivers being independent contractors. |

- In the above case the court set out the three conditions for someone to be an employee:
  - a person agrees to provide work and skill in return for a wage;
  - a person agrees, expressly or impliedly, to be under the employer's control;
  - the other terms are consistent with a contract of employment.
- This would include consideration of the following factors:
  - method of payment – if regular, an employee
  - tax – if deducted before payment, an employee
  - tools – if provided, an employee
  - business risks – if taken, an independent contractor
  - hours – if regular, an employee.
- In any particular case any of the above factors which are relevant are taken into account and a decision whether someone is an employee is made on balance. In some cases it may be argued either way.

## 12.2 Lending employees

- If an employer lends an employee to a second employer and the employee commits a tort, which employer is vicariously liable?
- The rules set out in the *Mersey Docks and Harbour Board* case took into account a number of factors but the presumption is that the original employer remains liable unless it was shown control had passed to the second employer.

| Case: | |
|---|---|
| *Mersey Docks and Harbour Board v Coggins & Griffiths* [1947] | MDHB hired out a driver and crane to C&G. While unloading a ship the driver negligently injured someone. Who was vicariously liable? The agreement between MDHB and C&G provided that the driver was an employee of C&G; C&G could tell the driver what to do; MDHB paid the driver and had power to dismiss him. The House of Lords said that MDHB still had greater control over the driver and remained his employer. |

- Recently, the courts have said that instead of choosing between two employers there can be **dual vicarious liability** in some situations.

V ———————————— TT

Subcontracted

**D Ltd** H [Supervisor of M+S]

**C AT** [M+S - workers with M controlling S's work]

| Case: | |
|---|---|
| ***Viasystems Ltd v Thermal Transfer Ltd* [2005]** | V contracted with TT to instal air conditioning in a factory. TT sub-contracted work to D Ltd, who in turn sub-contracted to CAT, who provided fitters. Two of the fitters, M and S, were working under the supervision of H who worked for D Ltd. S damaged the sprinkler system and flooded the factory. V claimed D Ltd and CAT were vicariously liable for the action of S. The Court of Appeal said that the important factor was the right of control and who was responsible for preventing the negligent act. Both H and M had the right to control S, therefore there was dual vicarious liability and both of them were liable. |

### Workpoint

Aimi runs a mobile hairdressing business. Beth works for Aimi. Aimi provides the clients and pays Beth for each client. Aimi also provides a uniform for Beth. Beth provides her own scissors and equipment, her own car and she is responsible for paying her own tax.

Cyril works as a nurse at the Dee NHS Hospital for three days per week. The other two days he works at the Exe private hospital. When he arrives at each hospital he is told what his duties are for the day.

Explain if Beth and Cyril are employees.

## Checkpoint – employees/independent contractors

| Task | Done |
|------|------|
| I can define the control test | |
| I can define the organisation test | |
| I can explain the economic reality test | |
| I understand *Ready Mix Concrete v MPNI* (1968) | |
| I can explain when dual vicarious liability can arise | |

# 12.3 Tort committed in the course of employment

- The employer will only be liable for torts committed 'in the course of employment'. The test used to decide this is known as the Salmond Test and was first set out by Professor Salmond in 1907:

  1. Is there a wrongful act which is authorised by the employer? or

  2. Is it a wrongful and unauthorised way of doing an authorised act?

- The House of Lords changed the second part of the test in *Lister v Hesley Hall* [2001] and the new test is whether there is a close connection between the employee's tort and their job.

- If the employer asks the employee to commit a tort (i.e. authorises it) then the employer will be liable.

- If there is a close connection between the tort and the job the employer will be liable.

| Case: | |
|-------|--|
| ***Century Insurance v Northern Island Road Transport Board* [1942]** | The defendants employed a tanker driver to deliver petrol. While delivering petrol the driver lit a cigarette and threw away the match causing an explosion. It was held that as he was doing this while delivering petrol he was acting within the course of his employment. His employer was vicariously liable. |

## 12.3.1 Express prohibition

- If the employer expressly prohibits a certain act and the employee does such an act it does not mean that the employer is not liable.

Otherwise the employer could simply tell the employee not to commit any torts!

- The employer can limit the scope of employment (what the employee does) but a limit on the method of employment (how the employee does the job) will not be effective.

| Case: | |
|---|---|
| **Limpus v London General Omnibus Co (1862)** | The defendant company told their bus drivers not to race other buses. A driver was racing another bus and caused an accident which damaged the claimant's bus. It was held that the driver was doing something he was authorised to do, driving the bus and although it was in an improper way, he was acting within the course of his employment. |

- This case can be contrasted with *Beard v London General Omnibus Co* [1900] in which the bus company were not vicariously liable for an accident caused by a bus conductor driving the bus. This was not within the course of employment.

- If an employee is told not to give lifts but does so and causes injury to a passenger, will the employer be vicariously liable? The cases have not been consistent.

| Case: | |
|---|---|
| **Twine v Beans Express [1946]** | The defendants told their employees not to give lifts. An employee gave someone a lift but crashed and the passenger was killed. The court said that giving a lift was unauthorised and outside the course of employment, therefore the defendant was not vicariously liable. |

- This can be contrasted with the decision in the next case.

| Case: | |
|---|---|
| **Rose v Plenty [1976]** | A milkman was told not to give anyone a lift on his milk float. He paid the 13-year-old claimant to help him and the claimant was injured due to the milkman's negligent driving. The court said that the prohibition only affected the way he did the job not what he had to do. The prohibited act was a benefit to the employer and was within the course of employment. |

- These two cases are contradictory and may only be distinguished by the fact that giving a lift against instructions was a benefit to the employer in one case (*Rose*) but not the other.

## 12.3.2 Criminal acts

- Can an employer be held vicariously liable for a criminal act by an employee? The employee can be prosecuted under the criminal law. If the criminal act is also a tort then the employer may be vicariously liable for that tort in civil law.

- For example:

  - a criminal assault will also be the tort of battery

  - a crime of theft will be the tort of conversion

  - a criminal fraud will be the tort of deceit (or fraud).

- The courts have had difficulty in deciding what criminal conduct is within the course of employment and what is outside it.

| Case: | |
|---|---|
| *Lloyd v Grace Smith & Co* [1912] | A solicitor's clerk fraudulently tricked a client into conveying her house to him. Although he did not have authority to defraud clients, conveyancing was part of his job and his employer was held to be vicariously liable. |

- The Court of Appeal held that sexual abuse by a head teacher was outside the course of employment as it could not be an unauthorised way of doing the job and the school were not vicariously liable (*Trotman North Yorkshire County Council* [1999]). The House of Lords reconsidered the position in Lister.

| Case: | |
|---|---|
| *Lister v Hesley Hall Ltd* [2001] | G was a warden at the defendant's boarding school for boys with behavioural problems. G sexually abused some boys. Under the *Salmond test* it could not be argued this was merely an unauthorised way of doing his job. The House of Lords said the test should be whether there was a 'very close connection' between the tort and the job. G's job was to look after the boys, he committed the abuse during his working time and on the defendant's premises. The defendants were held to be vicariously liable. |

- The test of a close connection has been applied in later cases.

| Case: | |
|---|---|
| **Mattis v Pollock [2003]** | The defendant owned a night club. He employed a bouncer to keep order and encouraged him to do this in an aggressive way. One night the bouncer's aggressive behaviour led to a fight involving the claimant. The bouncer left the club, went to his flat nearby and obtained a knife. He returned, saw the claimant standing in the street and stabbed him. The Court of Appeal said that the stabbing was not a separate incident and there was a close connection between the stabbing and the bouncer's job. The defendant was vicariously liable for the bouncer's actions. |

| Case: | |
|---|---|
| **Maga v Birmingham Roman Catholic Archdiocese Trustees [2010]** | The claimant was sexually abused in the 1970s by Father Clonan, a Catholic priest employed by the defendants. The claimant was not a Catholic but attended discos in the church community centre. He did jobs for Father Clonan including washing his car and cleaning his house. The abuse took place in the priest's house and in his car. The High Court held that although Father Clonan's position as a priest gave him the opportunity to abuse the claimant this was not sufficient to make the defendant vicariously liable and the jobs the claimant did were not connected to the priest's work. The Court of Appeal disagreed. They said that Father Clonan dressed as a priest; part of his duties was to befriend non-Catholics; he had responsibility for youth work; the discos were held on church premises; the claimant did work in the priest's house which was owned by the defendant; and abuse took place in the priest's house. The abuse was 'so closely connected' with his employment as a priest that the defendants were vicariously liable. |

- The courts have been heavily influenced by policy reasons in many cases e.g. to compensate the victims of abuse. The result is that in some cases it makes it difficult to determine if someone committing a criminal offence is acting within the course of employment.

# 12.3.3 A frolic of their own

- An employer will not be liable for torts committed by an employee when the employee is on a 'frolic of their own'. This will be treated as outside the course of employment. It often involves an employee travelling in the employer's vehicle and deviating from the route. It is not easy to determine this question as a comparison of the following cases will show. Each situation will have to be judged on its particular facts.

| Case: | |
|---|---|
| **Hilton v Thomas Burton [1961]** | Some workmen used their employer's van to go to a café for tea. They travelled seven or eight miles from their site but then changed their minds and turned back. On the return journey, due to the negligence of the driver they crashed and one of them was killed. It was held that they were on a frolic of their own and the defendants were not vicariously liable. |

| Case: | |
|---|---|
| **Harvey v O'Dell [1958]** | Some workmen travelled five miles from their site for lunch. There was an accident and one was injured. There was no canteen on site and it was held that the journey was in the course of employment and the employer was liable. |

## Research Point

Please read the following article: Scorer, R. (2010) Personal injury: Sins of the past, 160 *NLJ* 789.

Explain the significance of the decisions in *Lister v Hesley Hall* (2002), *A v Hoare* (2008) and *Maga v Birmingham Archdiocese* (2010) for someone bringing a claim under the principle of vicarious liability.

## Workpoint

Flo works as a sales representative for Makeitup, a cosmetics firm. She is provided with a company van but instructed not to give lifts to anyone during working hours. One day in between appointments she picks up her daughter, Gigi, from school. On the way home due to Flo's negligent driving, she crashes the van and Gigi is injured.

*Continued overleaf*

## Workpoint continued

Hari is a geography teacher at the Ivy Private School. He took a group of 16-year-old pupils on a camping trip to the coast for two days. Hari drove them in the school minibus. On returning from the trip he dropped off all the pupils and the other teacher at school. However, because it was nearly 10.00pm he agreed to give one pupil, Jane, a lift to her home. On the way Hari stopped the minibus and sexually assaulted her.

Explain (i) whether Flo is acting in the course of employment; and (ii) whether Hari is acting in the course of employment.

## Checkpoint – in the course of employment

| Task | Done |
|---|---|
| I can explain the *Salmond test* and how it has changed | |
| I can distinguish between *Twine* (1946) and *Rose* (1976) | |
| I can explain the test of close connection | |
| I understand what is meant by 'a frolic of their own' | |

# 12.4 Employer's indemnity

- The employer and the employee are jointly liable for the tort which has been committed. The claimant will usually sue the employer. However, the employer has a right of indemnity which means they can reclaim the damages paid from the employee. The employer may claim at common law under the principle in *Lister v Romford Ice*.

| Case: | |
|---|---|
| **Lister v Romford Ice [1957]** | A father and son both worked for the defendant. The son was parking his lorry and negligently knocked down and injured his father. The father sued the defendant under the principle of vicarious liability. The defendant then sued the son. It was held by the House of Lords that the son was in breach of an implied term in his contract of employment that he would use reasonable care. The defendant was entitled to be paid back by the son. |

- After this case insurers agreed not to use this right to claim from employees.

- As an alternative to claiming under *Lister* the employer has a right under the Civil Liability (Contribution) Act 1978 s1 to claim a contribution from any other person liable. Under s2(1) the amount is what the court deems just and equitable. This amount claimed may not be the full amount if the employer is partly to blame for the accident.

# 12.5 Independent contractors

- An employer is not liable for a tort committed by an independent contractor who carries out work for the employer. The independent contractor is liable for their own torts.

- **Point to note:** When answering problem questions if you decide that someone who commits a negligent act is not an employee, so vicarious liability does not arise, remember to consider their individual liability.

## 12.5.1 Exceptions

- If the employer owes a non-delegable duty. This is a duty which the employer cannot delegate legal responsibility for, even though they can delegate carrying out the work to an independent contractor.

- Examples would be:

  - Carrying out work on public roads

  - Very dangerous acts e.g. *Bottomley v Todmorden Cricket Club* [2003].

- If the employer authorises the independent contractor to commit a tort.

## Research Point

Look up the following article: Glassbrook, A. (2005) "You're only supposed to blow the bloody doors off!" – employers' vicarious liability for the torts of violent employees, JPIL.

The law has to decide whether there is a close connection between the tort and the job in cases of violent conduct.

1) Explain any three factors which are relevant in deciding.

2) Explain how the law deals with employees who are permitted to use force and those who are not.

## Potential exam question

'*The law on vicarious liability is not based on any clear principles or policy and is therefore difficult to apply in any particular case*'.

Discuss in relation to the liability of an employer for the acts of an employee.

# Chapter 13
## Defamation

## 13.1 Introduction

- Defamation protects a person's reputation. The rules of defamation must be considered in conjunction with the European Convention on Human Rights, in particular Article 10 – the right to freedom of expression – and Article 8 – the right to private life – which have been incorporated into English law by the Human Rights Act 1998.

- Claims for defamation are heard by a jury. If the claim is for under £10,000 then the case can be heard by a judge without a jury.

- A claim for defamation must be brought within one year (Limitation Act 1980 s4A).

- A claim for defamation ends with the claimant's death.

- How far the tort of defamation is successful in protecting reputation is a debateable point. It is often the case that an individual may be defamed in the press but cannot afford to take action for defamation against a powerful and wealthy business. State funding for legal claims does not apply to defamation. *Steel and Morris v UK* (2005) arose from libels published against McDonalds. The claimants were denied legal aid and largely represented themselves. It was held by the ECHR that this refusal of legal aid was a breach of Article 6 the right to a fair trial.

## 13.2 Libel and slander
### 13.2.1 Differences between libel and slander

| Libel | Slander |
|---|---|
| a statement in a permanent form | a statement in a temporary form |
| e.g. writing; picture; statue; film; words, pictures, images, broadcasts on radio or tv; statements in public plays | e.g. spoken statement; gesture |

| Libel | Slander |
|---|---|
| actionable *per se* – no need to prove damage | need to prove special damage; this is financial or material loss. Exceptions:<br>• committed a crime punishable by imprisonment<br>• suffers from a contagious disease<br>• unchastity of a woman<br>• unfit for any office, profession or business |
| a tort; but also a crime if it leads to a breach of the peace | a tort only |
| *Youssoupoff v MGM* [1934](CA) A film showed the claimant princess raped by Rasputin. Held that the pictures and speech were both libel. | |

# 13.3 Elements of defamation

> **Definition**
>
> Defamation: the publication of an untrue statement which lowers the claimant in the estimation of right-thinking members of society or causes them to be shunned or avoided (*Sim v Stretch* [1936]).

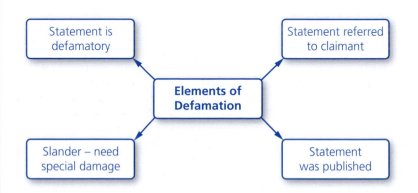

## 13.3.1 The statement is defamatory

- Words are given their ordinary meaning. For example, a false statement that someone was a rioter would be defamatory.

- The phrase 'right-thinking members of society' means the standard of a reasonable person which is an objective standard. This standard will change over time, for example, accusing someone of adultery is not viewed in the same way now as it was 40 years ago.

| Case: | |
|---|---|
| *Byrne v Deane* [1937] | A member of a golf club told the police about an illegal gambling machine at the club. The following poem then appeared on the wall in the club, 'But he who gave the game away, may he byrne in hell and rue the day'. The claimant sued the club for defamation. It was held that telling the police about an illegal gambling machine would not lower the claimant in the eyes of right-thinking members of society. The statement was not therefore defamatory. |

- If someone is rude and abusive to another person that will not normally be defamatory. But in *Berkoff v Burchill* [1996] the defendant described the claimant as 'hideous looking' and this was held capable of lowering the claimant in the eyes of the public as he made his living as an actor.

- Words or pictures which appear innocent may sometimes have a hidden meaning (or double meaning) – an innuendo. If other people know this meaning it will make it defamatory.

| Case: | |
|---|---|
| *Tolley v Fry* [1931] | The defendants published an advertisement for chocolate with the claimant's picture on it without his permission. This was not defamatory. The claimant was an amateur golfer which meant he was not paid. People who knew him would think he had been paid which made the advertisement defamatory. |

## 13.3.2 The statement referred to the claimant

- A statement which names the claimant or has their photograph meets this requirement.

- If the claimant is not named, the test is whether a reasonable person with knowledge of the facts would believe that the words referred to the claimant.
- There is no requirement that the defendant intended to defame the claimant. Defamation can happen by chance.

| Case: | |
|---|---|
| **Hulton v Jones [1910]** | The defendants published a fictional story about someone going on a trip to France with a woman who was not his wife. They made up a name for him, Artemus Jones. The claimant happened to be a barrister with that name. He proved that his friends thought the story was about him. It was held that the story was defamatory. |

- Even if an article is true of someone else it may still be defamatory of the claimant.

| Case: | |
|---|---|
| **Newstead v London Express Newspaper Ltd [1940]** | The defendants published a true report that Harold Newstead, a 30-year-old Camberwell man, had been convicted of bigamy. The claimant was also called Harold Newstead, was about 30 and lived in Camberwell. The claimant was able to show that people who knew him thought it was him. This was defamation. |

- Newspapers could avoid the above situation by giving the address of the person in the article.
- If a defamatory statement is made about a large group of people it will be difficult for one individual to bring a claim, for example 'All politicians are crooks'. It may be possible if the statement is about a small group (*Knuppfer v London Express Newspaper Ltd* [1994] (HL).

## 13.3.3 The statement was published

### 13.3.3.1 Published

- This requirement does not mean that the statement was published in the normal sense of being published in a book or a newspaper.

It simply means that the statement was made to a **third party** (i.e. someone apart from the claimant).

- 'Every new publication is a fresh libel' (Rule in *Duke of Brunswick v Harmer* (1849)).

  - Defendant tells their husband or wife – is not publication.

  - Defendant tells the claimant's husband or wife – is publication.

  - Letters – can amount to publication.

- If the defendant sends a defamatory letter to the claimant, that is not publication.

- But what if the letter is opened by someone else? The courts apply a test to ascertain whether it is reasonably foreseeable that someone else would see the letter.

- In *Theaker v Richardson* [1962] the defendant wrote a defamatory letter to the claimant and put it in a brown sealed envelope. The letter was opened by the claimant's husband who thought it was an election circular. It was held that this action was foreseeable and was publication. In contrast, a butler opening a letter was not foreseeable as it was not part of his duties and was not therefore published (*Huth v Huth* [1915]).

### 13.3.3.2 Internet

- If defamatory material is posted on an internet website the author will be the publisher. The internet service provider will not normally be the publisher as it plays a passive role in enabling use. The ISP could be treated as the publisher if it knew of the defamatory material and did not remove it within a reasonable time (*Godfrey v Demon Internet* [1999]).

### 13.3.3.3 Repetition

- If a third party repeats the defamatory statement the third party will be liable for a new publication.

- If it was foreseeable that the defamatory statement would be repeated by others the original defendant will be liable.

## 13.3.4 Slander – the claimant suffered special damage

- There is no need to prove damage in libel. In slander financial damage only needs to be shown in circumstances outside the exceptions (see 13.2 above).

## Workpoint

Abi, a television script writer, wrote an episode for a detective series in which a plumber called Jim Smith, who drove a red Ford van, murdered his wife. The episode was shown on Bee TV. Shortly after this they received an email from a Jim Smith, who was a plumber with a red Ford van. He said that his friends thought that the character in the detective series was him.

Carl lived in a village. There was a parish council of ten councillors which had been elected and had responsibility for the village. At a public meeting in the village hall Carl said, 'The parish council are all idiots. They couldn't organise a party in a brewery'.

Dai was away from home on a business trip. He sent an email to his wife, Ella, accusing her of having an affair with Fran, the next door neighbour. In error Dai also sent a copy of the email to Fran.

Explain whether the elements of defamation have been satisfied in the above situations and if so, the nature of that defamation.

## Checkpoint – elements of defamation

| Task | Done |
|---|---|
| I can define defamation | |
| I can distinguish libel and slander and give examples | |
| I can explain what 'right-thinking members of society' means | |
| I understand the decision in *Newstead v London Express Newspapers Ltd* (1940) | |
| I can explain who would be liable for a defamation posted on a website or social networking site | |

# 13.4 Defences to defamation

## 13.4.1 Offer of amends

- If the defamation has been made unintentionally the Defamation Act 1996 ss2–4 provides for a defence of 'offer to make amends' e.g. *Newstead v London Express Newspapers* [1940].

- This offer must:

  1. be in writing,

  2. publish a correction and apology in a reasonable way, and

  3. pay the claimant compensation and costs.

- Section 3 provides that if the offer is accepted the claimant cannot bring proceedings for defamation.

- Section 4 provides that if the offer is not accepted the fact that the offer was made is a defence to a defamation claim.

## 13.4.2 Justification

- If the defendant can prove that the statement is true, that is a good defence.

- The defendant only has to prove that the statement was 'substantially true' and not the fine detail of the statement.

| Case: | |
|---|---|
| *Alexander v North Eastern Rly Co* (1865) | The defendants put a notice up at the station that the claimant had been convicted of travelling without a ticket and fined £1 or three weeks' imprisonment if he did not pay. The actual sentence was two weeks' imprisonment. It was held that the defence of justification succeeded as the statement was substantially true. |

- The Defamation Act 1952 s5 deals with a statement which contains a number of defamatory remarks. The defence of justification will not fail if every remark is not proved, as long as those not proved do not materially injure the claimant's reputation with regard to the truth of the other remarks.

- For example, the defendant makes a statement that the claimant (1) stole £100,000 from a post office and at the same time (2) stole a bar of chocolate. The fact the defendant cannot prove (2) would not injure the claimant's reputation if (1) was proved and the defence of justification would succeed.

- If the defence of justification fails the claimant may be awarded higher damages.

## 13.4.3 Absolute privilege

- In some circumstances the right to freedom of expression is so important that a person making an untrue statement will not be liable in defamation. This applies even if the statement is made maliciously. This defence is important to allow people to carry out their roles without worrying about being sued for defamation, for example MPs speaking out about corruption or witnesses giving evidence in court.

### 13.4.3.1 Parliament

- Parliamentary privilege includes:

  - statements made in Parliament e.g. in committees

  - reports published by Parliament e.g. *Hansard.*

- It does not apply to statements made by MPs outside Parliament.

### 13.4.3.2 The courts and judicial proceedings

- Privilege includes:

  - statements made in courts, tribunals and similar bodies e.g. General Medical Council by e.g. lawyers, witnesses

  - statements made to lawyers for the purpose of proceedings

  - fair and accurate reports of court proceedings made soon afterwards.

### 13.4.3.3 Officers of state

- Privilege includes statements by government ministers.

- This does not apply to civil servants.

## 13.4.4 Qualified privilege

- This defence applies to a wider range of situations than absolute privilege. An important limitation is that the statement has to be made without malice and with a belief in its truth.

### 13.4.4.1 At common law

- There are two limbs to this defence:

  1. the person making the statement must have a legal, moral or social duty to make it; and

  2. the person receiving the statement must have a corresponding duty or interest to receive it.

| Case: | |
|---|---|
| **Watt v Longsdon** **[1930]** | L was a director of a company with a branch in Morocco. B was a manager and W was managing director. B sent a letter to L making defamatory allegations that W was often drunk and immoral. L gave copies of the letter to S, the chairman of the company, and to Mrs W. The allegations proved to be untrue. It was held: (i) letter from B to L: covered by qualified privilege as both had an interest in the company; (ii) letter from L to S: covered by qualified privilege because there was a duty to tell S; (iii) letter from L to Mrs W: no social or moral duty to tell her about unfounded gossip, and the defence failed. |

## 13.4.4.2 The *Reynolds* defence

| Case: | |
|---|---|
| **Reynolds v Times Newspapers** **[1999]** | The defendants published an article about the claimant, a former Irish Prime Minister, stating that he had misled the Irish Parliament. The defendants argued that 'political information' should be a special category of qualified privilege because they had a duty to report such things and the public had a duty to receive such information. The House of Lords said that the defence of qualified privilege did not apply, particularly because the defendant's article did not mention the claimant's explanation for his conduct. The House of Lords set out a number of factors which should be considered in deciding if there was a duty to tell the public about political information. |

- The factors:

1. The seriousness of the allegation. The more serious it is, the more the public are misinformed if it turns out not to be true.

2. The nature of the information and the extent to which it is a matter of public concern.

3. The source of the information. Is it from someone with direct knowledge?

4. The steps taken to check the information.

5. The status of the information.

6. The urgency of the matter. News may not be news for long.

7. Whether the claimant was asked to comment on the matter.

8. Whether the article included the claimant's side of the story.

9. The tone of the article.

10. The circumstances and timing of the publication.

- These factors are not exhaustive. Since *Reynolds* there have been a number of important cases giving guidance on how the factors apply.

| Case: | |
|---|---|
| ***Jameel v Wall Street Journal Europe Sprl (No 3) [2007]*** | The defendants posted an article on a website in the US which implied that the claimant was involved in funding a terrorist organisation. This article could be accessed in England and the claimant sued for defamation. The defendant claimed qualified privilege under *Reynolds* but this was rejected in the High Court and Court of Appeal because the defendant had not checked the story with the claimant and allowed him to comment. The House of Lords accepted the defence. They said that the ten factors in the *Reynolds* test did not have to be met but were a guide in determining whether the journalism was responsible. |

| Case: | |
|---|---|
| *Flood v Times Newspapers Ltd* [2010] | The defendant published an article in its newspaper and on its website which stated that the claimant, a police officer, was corrupt. The police investigated the allegations but found no evidence against the claimant. He sued for libel and the defendant claimed qualified privilege. The Court of Appeal said that the defendant had not taken sufficient steps to check that the allegations were true and the article was not 'responsible journalism'. Consequently the defence of qualified privilege failed. |

- The *Reynolds* defence is not limited to political matters but anything which is of public interest. In *Flood*, corruption in the police is a matter of public interest. The courts are trying to strike a balance between allowing journalists to report such issues but requiring them to take care to check the accuracy of stories to protect the reputation of the person in the story.

### 13.4.4.3 Under statute

- Under schedule 1 of the Defamation Act 1996 s15, the following are privileged unless the publication is made with malice:

  - reports of proceedings in Parliament

  - reports of courts.

- Under schedule 2, the following are privileged unless made with malice or the defendant does not give the claimant the chance to put their side of the story:

  - public meetings of councils, companies and other public bodies.

---

**Research Point**

Look up the following article: Dobson, N. (2011), Public: A Walk in the Park, 161 *NLJ* 201. Explain the decision in *Clift v Slough Borough Council* [2010] EWCA Civ 1484 and in particular the effect of Article 8 on the Council's defence of qualified privilege.

## 13.4.5 Innocent dissemination

- This defence protects mechanical distributors e.g. the printers and sellers of defamatory material. It was originally a common law defence but is now contained in the Defamation Act 1996 s1.

- The defendant must show:

  1. they are not the author, editor or commercial publisher;

  2. they took reasonable care in relation to the publication; and

  3. they did not know and had no reason to believe that what they did contributed to the publication of a defamation.

- In *Godfrey v Demon Internet* [2001] a defence under s1 failed because the defendant knew the defamatory material had been on the server for two weeks and they had not removed it.

## 13.4.6 Honest comment

- This defence was known as 'Fair Comment on a matter of public interest' until it was changed by the Supreme Court in *Spiller v Joseph* [2010].

- The defence allows people the right to comment but it is restricted by the following requirements.

### 13.4.6.1 Comment

- The statement must be comment not fact. It is sometimes difficult to make this distinction.

| Case: | |
|---|---|
| ***British Chiropractic Association v Singh* [2010]** | The defendant wrote an article in *The Guardian* newspaper stating there was 'not a jot of evidence' to support claims by the BCA that its members could treat a range of illnesses. The BCA sued for libel. The High Court said this statement meant that the BCA dishonestly promoted treatments and the statement was fact not opinion. The Court of Appeal disagreed and said that the statement there is 'not a jot of evidence' was an expression of opinion about the evidence available. The defence of fair comment could therefore apply. |

### 13.4.6.2 Honest

- The opinion must be honestly held, however prejudiced it may seem. Also it must not be made with malice. A person acts with malice if they do not have an honest belief in what was stated or they are motivated by spite.

### 13.4.6.3 In the public interest

- The comment must be made in the 'public interest'. This covers a wide range of issues including political matters, local authorities, plays, media broadcasts, etc.

# 13.5 Remedies

- The two main remedies are damages and injunctions (see Chapter 15).

# 13.6 Reform

- The Defamation Bill 2011 proposes to reform and modernise the law.

---

**Workpoint**

Greg is the editor of the *Daily Bugle*, a local newspaper. The paper publishes an article reporting rioting in the local town centre and stating that one of the rioters has been identified as Huw Jones from the town. Shortly after this Greg received a letter from a university student called Huw Jones who also lives in the town but who was on holiday abroad at the time of the riots.

Ivy is a Member of Parliament. She had recently had a relationship with Greg, the editor of the *Daily Bugle* which he had ended. Ivy gave evidence to a committee of the House of Commons which was investigating phone hacking. Ivy falsely told the committee that her phone had been hacked by a reporter from the *Daily Bugle*.

Janet owns a newspaper shop. A magazine called 'Big News' which was on sale in the shop had a defamatory article about Wayne Rooney.

Explain whether any defences are available to Greg, Ivy and Janet.

---

**Checkpoint – defences to defamation**

| Task | Done |
| --- | --- |
| I can list the requirements for an offer of amends to apply | |
| I understand what 'substantially true' means | |

## Checkpoint – continued

| | |
|---|---|
| I can explain what absolute privilege covers | |
| I can explain the two requirements for qualified privilege at common law | |
| I can list the requirements for innocent dissemination | |
| I can explain the three restrictions on honest comment | |

## Research Point

Look up the following article: Shaw, R. And Chamberlain, P. (2011), No alarms and no surprises, *Sol Jo* Vol 155/11, which is about the Defamation Bill.

Explain the proposals in outline.

Look up the following article, which deals with defences: Gleeson, T. (2006) He That Filches From Me My Good Name, 170 *JPN* 795.

Identify, from each of the defences explained, examples of how they have worked in practice.

Also read: Marsoof, A. (2011) Online Social networking and the Right to Privacy: The Conflicting Rights of Privacy and Expression, *Int J Law Info Tech*, 19(2):110.

Explain the problems of balancing the right to privacy and freedom of expression in the context of social networking sites.

## Potential exam question

Alan is the editor of the *Daily News*, a national newspaper. Ben, a Member of Parliament, is a married man and known for attending church regularly. Alan publishes an article in the newspaper stating that a number of MPs have claimed that Ben was having a sexual affair with his secretary. The article is also posted on the newspaper website.

Alan also repeats his allegation to Ben's wife, Eli, at a party.

Daisy, an MP, had recently had a sexual affair with Ben but he had ended the relationship. During a debate in the House of Commons on standards in public life, she calls Ben 'a hypocritical sex maniac who is not fit to be a Member of Parliament'.

Advise Ben of any action he may take in tort.

# Chapter 14
## General defences and limitation

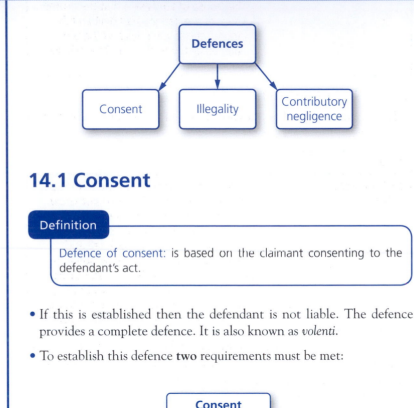

Defences

Consent    Illegality    Contributory negligence

## 14.1 Consent

> **Definition**
>
> Defence of consent: is based on the claimant consenting to the defendant's act.

- If this is established then the defendant is not liable. The defence provides a complete defence. It is also known as *volenti*.

- To establish this defence **two** requirements must be met:

Consent

Knowledge    Voluntary consent

## 14.1.1 Knowledge

- To give consent the claimant must know about the risk. But knowledge in itself is not enough and the claimant's conduct must show that they accept the risk.

| Case: | |
|---|---|
| *ICI v Shatwell* [1964] | The claimant and his brother worked at the defendant's quarry. The company rules stated that they had to use a shelter when testing explosives but they did not bother to use it and were both injured in an explosion. The claimant brother sued on the basis that the defendant was vicariously liable for his brother's actions. The House of Lords said that the brothers knew of the danger, had deliberately ignored the safety rules and therefore had consented to the risk. The defence failed. |

## 14.1.2 Voluntary consent

- Even if the claimant has full knowledge of the risk and consents, the consent must be voluntary.

| Case: | |
|---|---|
| *Smith v Baker* [1891] | The claimant worked for the defendant building a railway. The claimant knew that a crane swung rocks over his head. He complained to the employer but continued working. A rock fell and injured him. The employer argued that he had consented. The House of Lords said that he had not acted voluntarily and had not consented to the risk. He had no real choice but to keep working. |

- If the claimant has been drinking alcohol can they consent? It will depend oh how drunk they are. If they are very drunk and unable to understand the risk they cannot consent to it.

| Case: | |
|---|---|
| *Morris v Murray* [1990] | The claimant and defendant had been drinking all afternoon. The claimant then agreed to go flying in the defendant's plane, drove to the airfield and helped to start the plane. The plane crashed and the claimant was injured. The Court of Appeal said the claimant knew the pilot had drunk a considerable amount and the claimant accepted the risk. The defence of consent applied. |

- If the defendant is under a duty to prevent a person committing suicide but that person does so, can the defendant use the defence of consent?

- If the person is of unsound mind they cannot consent. In *Reeves v Metropolitan Police Commissioner* [2000] a prisoner, who was a known suicide risk but of sound mind, hanged himself. The House of Lords said that the police were under a duty to stop the prisoner committing suicide and the defence of consent failed. However, the prisoner was found to be 50% contributorily negligent.

## 14.1.2.1 Road traffic cases

- The defence of consent cannot be used in road traffic cases (Road Traffic Act 1988 s149).

## 14.1.2.2 Rescuers

- If a defendant negligently causes an accident and a rescuer goes to help and is injured, can the defendant use the defence that the rescuer consented?

- As a general rule the law will not treat rescuers as consenting (*Haynes v Harwood* [1935]).

### Workpoint

- Alan worked as a painter in a shipyard and often had to work at heights from a cradle which he stood in. Alan complained to Brian, the manager, that the cradle he was using had been damaged and wobbled when Alan stood in it. Brian said he would order a new one. The next day as the new cradle had not arrived Alan decided to use the damaged one. He was working 15 metres above the ground when the cradle wobbled and he fell and was injured.

- Dan took his girlfriend Cleo out for the evening and they both had six alcoholic drinks. When driving home, due to Dan's alcoholic state, the car overturned and Cleo was injured and trapped in the car. Eric, who was walking past, came to help Cleo and he was cut by broken glass.

Advise Brian and Dan whether or not they will be able to rely on the defence of consent.

### Checkpoint – consent

| Task | Done |
|---|---|
| I can explain the two requirements to establish consent | |
| I understand the effect of alcohol on consent | |

## Checkpoint – continued

| | |
|---|---|
| I can explain the decision in *Morris v Murray* (1990) | |
| I can explain the position in road traffic accidents as regards the defence of consent | |

# 14.2 Illegality

- If someone suffers harm while engaged in an illegal act they cannot sue in tort.

- The rule is based on public policy that it would be against the public conscience to allow claims in such circumstances. The principle is known as *ex turpi causa non oritur actio*. The classic example is the next case.

| Case: | |
|---|---|
| ***Ashton v Turner*** **[1981]** | The claimant and defendant were two burglars. While driving away from a burglary the defendant crashed and injured the claimant. The court rejected the claim because at the time of the injury the claimant was involved in a crime. |

- How the courts use this principle is not always clear. Two important factors are:

1. The connection between the criminal act and the harm – the closer the connection, the more likely it will be classed as illegal.

2. Whether the crime is major or minor – a major crime is more likely to result in the defence of illegality being available.

| Case: | |
|---|---|
| ***Vellino v Chief Constable of Greater Manchester Police*** **[2001]** | The police went to the claimant's second floor flat to arrest him. He tried to climb out the window, as he had done on previous occasions but fell and was paralysed. It was held that his injury was caused while he was committing a crime, evading lawful arrest and the illegality defence applied. His claim failed. |

| Case: | |
|---|---|
| **Pitts v Hunt [1990]** | After spending the evening drinking the claimant and defendant set off home. The claimant was a pillion passenger on the defendant's motorcycle. He knew the defendant had no licence or insurance. The defendant was weaving across the road and the claimant encouraged him to do this. The defendant collided with a car and was killed and the claimant was injured. The Court of Appeal said that the claimant had encouraged the defendant to commit illegal acts and this had caused the harm to the claimant. The defendant was not liable. |

| Case: | |
|---|---|
| **Gray v Thames Trains Ltd [2009]** | The claimant suffered post-traumatic stress disorder (PTSD) due to a train accident caused by the defendant. He later killed someone because of his condition, was convicted of manslaughter and detained in a secure hospital for an indefinite period. He sued for damages for PTSD and loss of earnings while he was detained. It was held that he was entitled to compensation only up to the time he was detained but at that point the defence of illegality applied. |

- The next case shows the limits of the illegality defence.

| Case: | |
|---|---|
| **Revill v Newberry [1996]** | The defendant, an old man, slept in his allotment shed to protect his property. When he heard the claimant trying to break in, he shot him through a hole in the door. The defendant put forward the defence of illegality. The court said that the defendant did owe a duty to the claimant and could not treat him as an outlaw so the defence of illegality failed. |

## Checkpoint – illegality

| Task | Done |
| --- | --- |
| I can explain the case of *Ashton v Turner* (1981) | |
| I can name the two factors relevant to establishing illegality | |
| I understand the decision in *Revill v Newberry* (1996) | |

# 14.3 Contributory negligence

- If a person suffers damage partly through their own fault and partly through the fault of another, the damages that person can recover shall be reduced to the extent a court thinks just and equitable.

## 14.3.1 The law reform (contributory negligence) act 1945 s1(1)

- The defence of contributory negligence is only a **partial** defence and the defendant will still have to pay some damages.

- The defendant must prove:

### 14.3.1.1 The claimant acted negligently

- The courts apply an objective standard to determine if the claimant's conduct was negligent.

| Case: | |
| --- | --- |
| ***Jones v Livox Quarries* [1952]** | The claimant was riding on the back of the defendant's traxcavator. It was hit from behind by another vehicle and the claimant was injured. A reasonable person would foresee that the risks included falling off and being hit from behind. It was held that the claimant was 20% contributory negligent. |

• This standard will not apply in certain circumstances.

## Children

• Children are judged by an ordinary child of that particular age. A young child will not be found contributory negligent. In *Yachuk v Oliver Blais & Co Ltd* [1949] the defendants sold petrol to the 9-year-old claimant. The claimant was burned playing with it but was not contributorily negligent.

| Case: | |
|---|---|
| **Gough v Thorne** **[1966]** | A 13-year-old girl was waiting to cross a busy road. A lorry driver stopped and indicated to her to cross. As she was crossing, a car overtook the lorry and hit the girl. The High Court found she was contributory negligent. The Court of Appeal said that she had been beckoned on by the lorry driver and relied on that. She was not contributory negligent. Denning LJ said that a child should only be contributorily negligent if they are 'of such an age as reasonably to be expected to take precautions for his or her own safety'. |

## Emergencies

• If the defendant negligently creates a danger the courts make allowance for actions in the heat of the moment.

| Case: | |
|---|---|
| **Jones v Boyce** **[1816]** | The claimant was sitting on top of the defendant's coach as it was going down hill. A defective rein broke and the claimant, thinking it would crash, jumped off and broke his leg. The coach did not crash. It was held that a reasonable and prudent person would have acted in the same way and the claimant was not contributorily negligent. |

• But compare this case to the following Canadian case.

| Case: | |
|---|---|
| *Holomis v Dubuc* [1975] | The claimant was a passenger in a sea plane. The defendant pilot landed on a lake in fog, hit an obstacle and the plane began to fill with water. Three passengers jumped out and one, the claimant's husband, drowned. It was held that jumping out in an emergency was not contributorily negligent but failing to put on the lifebelts which were available was. Damages were reduced by 50%. |

## 14.3.1.2 The claimant's act caused some damage

- The claimant's act must either partly cause the accident or must cause some of the damage.

| Case: | |
|---|---|
| *Froom v Butcher* [1976] | The claimant was in a car accident caused by the defendant's negligence. He was not wearing his seatbelt. Seatbelts were not compulsory at that time. He suffered head injuries which he would not have suffered if he had worn a seatbelt. It was held that he had been contributorily negligent and his damages were reduced by 20%. |

- Lord Denning said of this case:

*'But in seatbelt cases the cause of the accident is one thing. The cause of the damage is another. The accident is caused by the bad driving. The damage is caused in part by the bad driving of the defendant, and in part by the failure of the plaintiff to wear a seatbelt'.*

- Lord Denning set out guidance for the reduction in damages for not wearing a seatbelt:

1. 0% if it made no difference

2. 15% if the injury would have been less severe

3. 25% if the injury would have been prevented altogether.

- These are guidelines and will not be followed in exceptional cases e.g. if a passenger could show that if they had worn a seatbelt this would have caused greater injuries.

- These guidelines were applied to cycle helmets in the following case.

| Case: | |
|---|---|
| **Smith v Finch [2009]** | The claimant rode out of a side road on his bicycle and was hit by the defendant's motorcycle. The claimant suffered head injuries. The defendant argued that the claimant was contributorily negligent because he was not wearing a cycle helmet. There is no legal requirement to wear a helmet. It was held that on the evidence, in a collision at low speed, a helmet would make no difference. The claimant was not contributorily negligent. |

- A claimant cannot be 100% contributory negligent. In *Pitts v Hunt* [1990] the High Court had said that the claimant was 100% contributory negligent. The Court of Appeal said that this would mean that the claimant caused the accident.

## Workpoint

Frank went to a cricket match at his local cricket club. He drank a number of pints of beer and decided to take his jacket and shirt off. He then left the stand where he had been sitting and stood near the edge of the pitch. Giles, the batsman, hit the ball into the air and it struck Frank on his bare chest, breaking two of his ribs.

Haroon was giving his brother Jak a lift to the station to catch a train. Haroon was speeding, lost control of the car and it hit a lamppost. Jak, who was not wearing a seatbelt, was injured.

Advise Giles and Haroon of any defences they may have against claims in negligence.

## Checkpoint – contributory negligence

| Task | Done |
|---|---|
| I can name the two factors to establish contributory negligence | |
| I can explain the standard applied to children and give a supporting case | |
| I understand the effect of the claimant acting in an emergency | |
| I can distinguish between the cause of the accident and the cause of the harm | |

- It would be unjust if a claimant could sue a defendant many years after a tort was committed. The law sets time limits for bringing claims. The law is set out in the Limitation Act 1980 (as amended).

| | |
|---|---|
| s2 | General rule – claims in tort must be brought within six years of when the cause of action arises.<br><br>• If a tort is actionable on proof of damage the cause of action arises when the damage occurs e.g. negligence.<br>• If a tort is actionable *per se* (without proof of damage) the cause of action arises when the defendant commits the tort e.g. trespass to land. |
| s11 | BUT claims for personal injury due to negligence, nuisance or breach of duty must be brought within three years from when:<br><br>(a) the right of action arises; or<br>(b) the date the claimant has knowledge of the injury. |
| s14 | The date of knowledge is when the claimant first had knowledge:<br><br>• injury was significant<br>• injury was caused wholly or partly by the act or omission of the defendant (negligence, nuisance or breach of statutory duty)<br>• identity of the defendant<br>• if act was someone apart from the defendant the identity of that other person.<br><br>A claimant will be treated as having knowledge which the claimant would be able to obtain with or without professional help. |
| s4A | Defamation – claim must be made within one year from the defamation. |
| s11A | Defective products – claim must be within three years from when the cause of action arises or the date of knowledge of the claimant, if later.<br>Ten-year absolute stop on claims from when product supplied. |
| s1 | Death – Law Reform (Miscellaneous Provisions) Act 1934.<br>If a claimant dies as a result of a tort before the end of the three-year period the dependants have three years from that date to sue. |

- Extending the limitation period s33 provides that a court has a discretion to extend the limitation period. The court must consider all the circumstances:

1. length of delay by claimant and reasons

2. how the delay will affect the evidence

3. conduct of defendant after claim arose

4. how long any disability of the claimant has lasted

5. whether the claimant acted promptly when they knew they could sue

6. steps taken by the claimant to obtain advice.

- This section only applies to claims under s11 so that claims for torts actionable *per se* are not covered. The law was extended in the next case.

| Case: | |
|---|---|
| ***A v Hoare*** **[2008]** | The claimant sued for trespass 16 years after she was raped. The reason was that the defendant, who was responsible, had recently won £7m on the Lottery. Under s2 she had six years to claim but this period had passed. The House of Lords said that a claim for personal injury from an intentional trespass was within s11. As a result the court could extend the period under s33 and allowed her claim. |

## Latent damage

- Latent damage is damage which is hidden or cannot easily be detected e.g. defective foundations of a house. The problem this caused is illustrated in the following case.

| Case: | |
|---|---|
| ***Pirelli v Oscar Faber*** **[1983]** | The defendant designed a tall chimney for the claimants in 1969. Cracks developed near the top of the chimney in 1970 but were not seen until 1977. It was held that the claim failed because the six-year limitation period ran from 1970. |

- The Latent Damage Act 1986 amended the Limitation Act 1980. It applies to negligence claims but not to personal injuries.

- Under s14A, a claim must be brought within six years of when the cause of action arises or, if later, three years from when the claimant knew or should have known about the damage.

- Section 14B imposes a 15-year-long stop period from the date of the last act of negligence by the defendant.

## Checkpoint – limitation acts

| Task | Done |
|---|---|
| I can state the general limitation period for claims in tort | |
| I can state the limitation period for claims of personal injury | |
| I can explain when claims for personal injury can be brought under s11 | |
| I understand the circumstances in which the limitation period can be extended | |

## Research Point

Please read the following article: Patten, K. (2011) Personal Injury: Time Out?, 161 NLJ 1393.

(i) Explain the requirement that knowledge must be 'significant' for the three-year limitation period to run.

(ii) Explain how that requirement was applied in *Sir Robert Lloyd v Bernard Hoey* [2011] EWCA Civ 1060.

(iii) Explain whether you consider the decision is just and the effect of the decision on the need for the law to provide certainty.

## Potential exam question

Alan and his girlfriend Becca were in their mid-20s and both worked in banking in the city. Alan was made redundant and Becca took him out for a pub lunch to cheer him up. Becca also brought along her younger sister Cleo. They all had a leisurely lunch and drank a number of bottles of wine.

*Continued overleaf*

Alan then suggested going for a trip in his speedboat which was moored on the river. Alan said that he would drive them to the river in his car and Becca and Cleo agreed. As he approached the river, due to the effects of alcohol, he lost control of his car and it collided with a concrete barrier. Cleo, who was not wearing her seatbelt, was knocked unconscious and suffered a head injury.

Neither Alan nor Becca were hurt in the accident and, believing that Cleo had just fallen asleep, they went off to find the speedboat. Alan started the speedboat and was steering it along the river in a reckless manner when Becca thought that the speedboat was going to collide with an oncoming vessel. Becca jumped out of the boat into the river but in doing so Becca was badly injured. In fact the speed boat did not collide with the oncoming vessel.

Advise (i) Cleo and (ii) Becca of any claims they may make in negligence and of any defences which may be available.

# Chapter 15

# Remedies

## 15.1 Introduction

- The main remedies in tort are **damages** and **injunctions**. Damages are financial compensation. Injunctions are mainly to stop the defendant from continuing with the tort. There are other remedies which apply to particular torts.

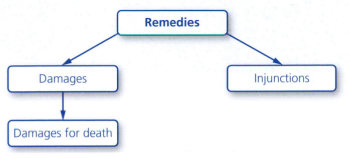

## 15.2 Damages

- Damages are compensation for the claimant. The aim of damages in tort is to put the claimant in the position they would have been in if the tort had not been committed. This principle is known as *restitutio in integrum*.

- A claimant is under a duty to mitigate his losses, which means they must take reasonable steps to reduce their losses.

### 15.2.1 Compensatory damages

- The purpose is to compensate the claimant for the loss they have suffered. The law cannot restore someone to their original position in all cases especially in the case of personal injuries e.g. if the claimant loses a leg in a car accident. Damages are the only means to provide some compensation.

- Compensatory damages can be divided into general damages and special damages.

#### 15.2.1.1 General damages

- General damages are damages which cannot be precisely measured e.g. damages for pain and suffering, or loss of future earnings.

### 15.2.1.2 Special damages

- Special damages are damages which can be precisely measured e.g. loss of earnings up to the trial.

## 15.2.2 Non-compensatory damages

- The main aim of these damages is not to compensate. They could be either more or less than compensatory damages.

### 15.2.2.1 Contemptuous damages

- This is a very small sum, usually the smallest coin, one penny. The court is saying that although there has been a technical breach of the law the case should not have been brought.

### 15.2.2.2 Nominal damages

- This is a small sum of money, awarded where the defendant has committed a tort but the claimant has not suffered any damage. They could be awarded for torts actionable *per se* like trespass to land e.g. £5.

### 15.2.2.3 Aggravated damages

- If the defendant has behaved in a way which causes mental distress or injury to the claimant's feelings, the court may give additional damages. In *Rowlands v Chief Constable of Merseyside* [2006] the claimant was wrongly arrested in a humiliating manner and she was awarded aggravated damages.

### 15.2.2.4 Exemplary damages

- The purpose of exemplary damages is to punish the defendant. In *Rookes v Barnard* [1964] the House of Lords said that such damages could only be awarded if:

  - there was oppressive, arbitrary or unconstitutional action by government servants e.g. they are abusing their power in some way, or

  - a defendant has committed a tort and calculated that they will make a profit e.g. publishing a book with libels believing it will make more money than damages awarded, *Cassell v Broome* [1972] (HL).

### 15.2.2.5 Claims for personal injury

- A claim for personal injury, both physical and psychiatric, is more difficult to assess than a claim for damage to property. With property damage the claimant can usually be given the replacement cost or the cost of repair.

- Losses can be divided into pecuniary (or financial) loss and non-pecuniary loss.

*Pecuniary (financial) loss*

- Pecuniary losses are:

  - Reasonable expenses e.g. private medical expenses are allowed;

  - Loss of earnings up to the trial;

  - Loss of future earnings: multiplicand (annual net earnings) × multiplier (years loss will continue);

  - Loss of earning capacity e.g. if claimant has to take a lower-paid job;

  - If life is shortened a claim for 'lost years' the claimant would have worked;

  - Cost of a carer if necessary (either professional or family).

*Non-pecuniary loss*

- Non-pecuniary losses are:

  - Pain and suffering: pain, from the actual injury and medical treatment; and suffering, from distress and disruption to life caused by the injury;

  - Loss of amenity: this is a claim for not being able to live life to the full after the accident, e.g. no longer play sports or enjoy leisure interests.

## Checkpoint – damages

| Task | Done |
|---|---|
| I can distinguish general and special damages | |
| I can name and explain the four types of compensatory damages | |
| I can explain what financial loss covers | |
| I can explain what pain, suffering and loss of amenity cover and give my own examples of them | |

# 15.3 Death

## 15.3.1 Claim by the estate

- If the claimant dies before the case reaches court, the Law Reform (Miscellaneous Provisions) Act 1934 s1(1) provides that all claims by (or against) the deceased survive for the benefit of the estate. The estate is what someone leaves after their death. Whoever inherits the estate will be able to claim for the losses up to the death. They claim as the representative of the deceased. The claim covers both pecuniary and non-pecuniary losses.

## 15.3.2 Claim by dependants

- If a person dies, as a result of a tort, anyone who was financially supported by the deceased may make a claim against the defendant under the Fatal Accidents Act 1976 s1. This is a claim by the dependant for the loss which they have suffered as a result of the death caused by the defendant.

- The list of **dependants** is set out under s1(3) and includes:

  - spouse or former spouse

  - civil partner or former civil partner

  - anyone who has lived with the deceased for two years before death as spouse or civil partner

  - parents

  - children including anyone treated as a child of the family

  - children of brothers, sisters, uncles and aunts

  - stepchildren

  - illegitimate children.

- The main claim is for the financial loss caused to the dependant e.g. if a parent is killed, the loss of their income less their expenses.

## 15.3.3 Bereavement damages

- Section 1A provides for damages to be given for bereavement.

These can only be claimed by:

  - the spouse or civil partner of the deceased

  - the parents of a minor who was never married or in a civil partnership.

- The amount given is a fixed sum which is currently £11,800.

### Workpoint

Amanda is 20 years old and works as a legal executive. She is crossing the road at a controlled crossing when Bob, who is not keeping a look out, drives through the red light. He knocks Amanda over and breaks her leg and she is taken to an NHS hospital for treatment. As a result of the accident she is off work for six weeks and is told that she will not be able to play netball for her local team for the rest of the season. As Amanda is not able to look after herself her mother Carol has to come and stay with her to look after her.

Dave lives next door to Eric. A passage way runs between their houses and they both have a right to use it. However, Eric often leaves his ladders leaning against the wall of Dave's house. Dave has asked him not to do this but he continues to do so. Dave decides to sue Eric for trespass to land.

Frank is a 40-year-old electrician and earns £40,000 a year. He is married to Gill and they have two children, Hari, aged three, and Irene, aged six. Frank is driving his family to the shops when a car driven by Jon suddenly crosses the centre of the road and hits Frank's car head on. Jon was using his mobile phone and lost control of his car. Frank and Hari were killed instantly but Gill and Irene escape injury.

Explain what damages may be claimed by:

(a) Amanda;

(b) Dave;

(c) Gill.

# 15.4 Injunctions

- An injunction is a court order stopping the defendant from doing something or ordering the defendant to do an act.

- It is an equitable remedy and will only be granted at the discretion of the court. It will not be given if damages are an adequate remedy.

## 15.4.1 Types of injunction

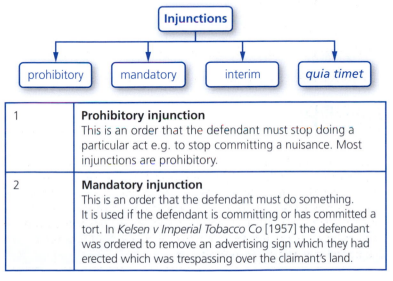

| 1 | **Prohibitory injunction** <br> This is an order that the defendant must stop doing a particular act e.g. to stop committing a nuisance. Most injunctions are prohibitory. |
|---|---|
| 2 | **Mandatory injunction** <br> This is an order that the defendant must do something. It is used if the defendant is committing or has committed a tort. In *Kelsen v Imperial Tobacco Co* [1957] the defendant was ordered to remove an advertising sign which they had erected which was trespassing over the claimant's land. |

| 3 | **Interim injunction**<br>An interim injunction (or interlocutory) is issued between the start of the case and the trial e.g. to stop the defendant continuing to commit a nuisance such as making noise. |
|---|---|
| 4 | ***Quia timet* injunction**<br>This is granted to stop a tort being committed e.g. the defendant is threatening to dig a ditch on the claimant's land. This is a very unusual remedy. |

## Checkpoint – death and injunctions

| Task | Done |
|---|---|
| I can identify the three possible claims arising in the event of death | |
| I can list the dependants under the Fatal Accidents Act 1976 | |
| I can name the four types of injunction | |
| I can explain the four types of injunction and give an example of when they will be used | |

## Research Point

Please read the following article: Scorer, R. (2010) Personal Injury: Where the Heart Is, 160 *NLJ* 1284.

(i) Explain what happens to damages which are awarded for care provided free by a family member for the victim of negligence.

(ii) Explain the decision in *Drake & Starkey v Foster Wheeler Ltd* [2010] EWHC 2004 (QB) and its effect on claims for the cost of care which has been provided for free.

## Potential exam question

Alex, aged 25, is a premiership footballer. He lives in a large house which has a swimming pool in the garden. His girlfriend Bev and their one-year-old daughter, Cath, live with him.

Daljit lives next door to Alex. A few weeks ago Daljit started clearing his house and burning rubbish in his garden. He lit fires every few days. Thick smoke from the fires drifted into Alex's house and ash landed in the swimming pool. Daljit has also erected a wind turbine, which is five metres high, close to the fence with Alex's garden. When the wind turbine is operating the blades pass over the boundary into Alex's airspace.

Two weeks ago Eric, a farmer, was driving his tractor through the village at high speed. He lost control of the tractor and it suddenly crossed the middle of the road and collided with Alex's sports car. Alex was unable to avoid the collision. Alex suffered broken ribs and a broken leg as a result of the impact. He was taken to hospital for treatment and was in pain for a week. Doctors had to amputate his damaged leg. As a result he is unable to play football again and has found a job as a sports reporter on his local newspaper at a modest salary. He is unable to continue his hobby of ballroom dancing.

(i) Advise Alex of the remedies he may obtain in respect of the above torts.

(ii) Assume Alex was killed in the accident. Advise Bev of any claim she may have in respect of the traffic accident only.

# Glossary

**Assault** an act which causes another person to apprehend the infliction of immediate, unlawful, force on his person

**Battery** the direct application of unlawful force to another person, e.g. punching someone

**Bolam test** a person with a particular skill must reach the standard of an experienced competent person with that skill

**Consent (or *volenti*)** is a defence that the claimant consented to the defendant's act; it is a complete defence

**Contributory negligence** an act by the claimant which contributes to the claimant's harm; it is a partial defence and the claimant's damages are reduced

**Defamation** the publication of an untrue statement which lowers the claimant in the estimation of right-thinking members of society or causes them to be shunned or avoided

**Duty of care** to establish this, the requirements of foreseeability, proximity and fair, just and reasonableness must be met

**Economic loss** financial loss which does not arise from injury, death or damage to property.

***Ex turpi causa non oritur actio*** no claim can be based on an illegal act

**False imprisonment** stopping someone moving freely without a lawful justification

**Fault liability** someone is only liable if they are at fault in some way, e.g. acting negligently

**Libel** defamation in a permanent form usually printed, but also includes paintings, statues and waxworks. It also includes defamation in broadcasts or stage plays

**Negligent act** an act which is in breach of a duty of care

**Negligent mis-statement** a careless statement which results in loss to the claimant

***Novus actus interveniens*** a new intervening act which breaks the chain of causation so that the defendant is not liable

**Primary victim** someone who is directly involved and within the range of foreseeable personal injury

**Private nuisance** an unlawful act which indirectly causes physical damage to land or interferes with enjoyment of land, or interferes with interests in land, and which is unreasonable taking into account all the circumstances

**Public nuisance** an act or omission 'which materially affects the reasonable comfort and convenience of life of a class of Her Majesty's subjects'

***Res ipsa loquitur*** means the thing speaks for itself; the result is that there is no need to prove negligence

**Secondary victim** someone not directly involved but who suffers from what they see or hear.

**Slander** defamation in a temporary form e.g. speech or gestures

**Strict liability** even though someone has not done anything wrong (i.e. there is no fault) they are liable

**Tortfeasor** a person who commits a tort

**Trespass to land** a direct and unlawful interference with another person's possession of land

**Vicarious liability** the rule that one person is liable in tort for the actions of another

# Index